RANDALL MILITARY MODELS

Fighters, Bowies and Full Tang Knives

by Robert E. Hunt

TURNER PUBLISHING COMPANY

CONTENTS

ACKNOWLEDGMENTS 4

CONTRIBUTORS 4

CHAPTER ONE: FIGHTERS 7

CHAPTER TWO: FIGHTING STILETTOS 52

CHAPTER THREE: FULL TANG KNIVES OF THE VIETNAM ERA 81

CHAPTER FOUR: CARRIED KNIVES 117

CHAPTER FIVE: BOWIE KNIVES 177

CHAPTER SIX: SETS 213

CHAPTER SEVEN: SHEATHS 255

CHAPTER EIGHT: LETTERS 283

INDEX 300

www.turnerpublishing.com

Copyright © 2003 Robert Hunt
Publishing Rights: Turner Publishing Company

This book or any part thereof may not be reproduced without the
written consent of Robert Hunt and Turner Publishing Company.

Library of Congress Control Number:
2003115697

ISBN: 978-1-56311-953-8

Printed in the United States of America.
Limited Edition

978-1-62045-511-1 (pbk.)

INTRODUCTION

Randall Fighting Knives in Wartime provided me with an opportunity for further study on this subject as well as serving to enhance the pleasure that goes along with accumulating a collection. Many others share this appeal and that circumstance, coupled with the positive reception of this first book, led directly to the formulation of *Randall Military Models*.

It was clear long before the first book was published that the subject matter could not be exhausted. On the contrary, three major wars and one-half century of fighting knife production left a great deal unsaid about Randall Military models, especially those that had been carried and used in a wartime theater of operations. That period must also account for thousands of military knife collectors, many of whom have owned, carried, and used a Randall-Made fighting knife; some in the service of their country.

In *Randall Military Models* I have attempted to continue the process of identifying, describing and dating fighting knives that were produced in the dramatic early days of the Bo Randall experience. However, the approach to this volume is different from the last. A change in formatting has permitted grouping of similar type(s), which has led to a section comparing like knives in pairs, sets and groups for the reader to study.

The "Fighter" has a section devoted to this well-known design, as does the "Fighting Stiletto", equally famous in its own right. The Vietnam period full-tang models are featured together, drawing attention to that unique design that spawned no less than five important period fighters twenty years after the introduction of the Model 1 and 2.

Bowie knives, passionately collected by some and sometimes carried during a war or national crisis, have received a section of their own that I hope many will find interesting and informative. The early Bowie years, 1953-1954, produced the same innovations identifiable in those blades that WW II knives reflected during 1943 and 1944, when function dictated design.

The heart of this book, however, is the section on "carried pieces," which features Randalls that have at least one of the several distinguishing requirements qualifying it to be considered a military model used in wartime. This section has over twenty-five examples, most never before photographed, that will introduce (to many for the first time), the attraction of the "used" knife, which is, after all, prototypical for the unused collectors knives that crowd the argyles in our dresser drawers.

The presentation of these many examples, accompanied by informative text and medium format photography, represents a definitive study. Unlike *Randall Fighting Knives*, where the large majority of knives depicted were from the author's personal collection, this book has permitted many friends and fellow collectors to contribute a knife or two. This has led to discovery and a shared common study that has furthered the project. Each contributor is identified along with the photograph of his knife.

New information continues with a section on RMK sheaths, which centers on full image examples that are sometimes difficult to identify (and collect).

The closing chapter depicts original previously unpublished correspondence from Bo Randall describing some of his views and recollections on product development during the early days of his knife-making career.

Depicting a knife in a photograph so that it will repeatedly hold a viewer's interest time and again, is challenging. The photograph takes us out of the realm of three dimensions so the picture remains fixed; we can't pick it up and look at it from another angle.

The inclusion of background material results in a "composition" that should serve to bring out the best in the subject and also enhance the overall image. Some photographs in this book depict the knife on a simple mat background, and this may be best to show that knife, but the final composition for a military knife begs to be supported by material and equipment that creates an image of relevance in time and place.

Randall Military Models is designed to have over 300 pages and approximately 150 full-page color photographs, accompanied with informative text. Like the first volume, it does not exhaust the subject, yet provides a vast amount of material, carefully organized and presented to enable the reader to further his own research in the areas most interesting to him.

Finally, I, like many of you, eagerly look forward to the release of this volume and to the continued study and circulation of accurate information relating to the collecting of Randall Fighting Knives.

Robert Hunt

ACKNOWLEDGMENTS

This book is dedicated to the Randall knife collector and to the many friends who we can attribute a knife or two, which appear in *Randall Military Models*. These contributors are listed below in alphabetical order and once again after the text opposite the photograph of their knife. The interaction with these collectors has made the investment in time a great pleasure as well as a reciprocal learning experience. It has also served to create a broader base of interest within this specialized collecting field.

Considerable time and effort was expended in photographing the 150 knives depicted. My friend and tutor Paul Liebenberg weaned me from the 35MM and introduced me to medium format photography. The results speak for themselves.

Photographic processing, scanning and digital images were prepared by Com Color, Springfield, Massachusetts.

Julie Murkette, who monitors and updates my web site, typed the text and prepared the final package for submission to Turner Publishing Company.

Keith Steele, along with Charlotte Harris at Turner's, maintained an open door after publication of the first book and paved the way for the second. Special recognition goes to Shelley Davidson for her creativity in design and layout in both volumes.

Finally, text review has fallen to Sara Hunt, who patiently read and critiqued the narratives written for each photograph.

The Author

CONTRIBUTORS

Donald Anderson, Ronnie Beckett, John Cheek, Gary Colpitts, Peter Cuervo, John Edwards, Ron Frumkes, Peter Hagen, Dave Harmon, Stan Kanakarus, Bob King, Bob Konior, Evan Nappan, Paul O'Connell, Dick Raynor, Walter Rhyne, Jeff Saucier, Chuck Shipman, Doug Smith, George Torres, Bob Tronolone, Walter Vedock

DO OR DIE – MANUAL ON INDIVIDUAL COMBAT
LT. COLONEL A. J. DREXEL BIDDLE U.S.M.C.R. (AS FEATURED ON THE COVER)

Long before Rex Applegate's *Kill or Get Killed*, and prior to WW II, Lt. Colonel Biddle had prepared a *Manual on Individual Combat*, which was accepted for training by the US Marine Corps. A career Marine Officer, Biddle was accomplished with the bayonet, broadsword, epee, knife and his hands. A proponent of individual training for combat, he stressed that the role of the infantryman would require personal tactics at close quarters in order to ensure survival and victory on the field of battle.

Interestingly enough, Biddle credited another Colonel, James Bowie, for developing techniques with the knife that he himself would eventually incorporate into "modern" combat training. The Bowie knife as well, developed on the American Frontier, was considered by him to be a far superior fighting weapon than any of its predecessors.

This author concurs, and although we cannot agree on an exact replication of the "original" Bowie knife, we can certainly find dozens of types that were carried and used during that wild period of our National expansion.

Here's a knife that would satisfy the requirements of any serious proponent of "knife defense," back then or now, and would have been an ideal weapon for utilizing the techniques that Colonel Biddle furthered back in the late 1930s while preparing his young Marines for combat, close and personal.

Chapter One
FIGHTERS

It is not the purpose of this book to make a case for any one particular knife design over all others; but as a matter of historical note, that has already been done. Believe it or not, the Model 1 fighter has been around for sixty years now, and the design and maker's name are well recognized. Included on the following pages are photographs of a representative number of these all-purpose fighting knives. We hope to provide the many collectors of this most "original American" modern fighting knife style, a further opportunity to study many previously unpublished photographic examples, sequentially arranged in this section.

Also included are a few Springfield Fighters, the finished product of which was copied from a Randall fighter prototype with the approval of the original designer. The result was a carefully detailed reproduction of the original and a portion of this "fame" has carried over to the "Springfield Randall." At a time when government priorities restricted manufacturing of anything not directly connected to the war, the Randall-Larson endeavor was to assist in producing quality knives during the height of the war.

RANDALL COMMANDO WW II FIGHTER

This is the Randall "Commando" knife, so called by Bo himself when he devised one of his earliest fighter designs. Influences on the maker had to include the various "hunters and skinners" that he had produced in the early years of development just prior to WW II. The blade style in particular, with its upswept tip, favors skinning knives. The shape of the sheath bears this out.

It has been speculated that this may have been the first fighter type, and this example does exhibit the hallmarks of early production.

Beginning with the blade we can observe the flat sides and "subtle" grind lines. The top is beveled and then sharpened from the tip 3 inches rearward toward the guard, obviously designed with back cutting in mind. The top line of this 6 7/8-inch blade is not radical and sweeps from tip to guard with only a slight rise where the sharpened clip meets the spine. This appears to be an early adaptation as later versions, some with wrist thong holes, exhibit a hump on the spine where the bevel meets the sharpened edge. Reference the "little commando" depicted in this section, which is a somewhat later knife with prominent hump on the blade back. Apparently this design was modified, as were all others, even in the brief span of its limited production. Also see a similar type in a larger version in *Randall Fighting Knives*, page 27, which has been attributed to 1944 production.

The blade on this knife is well preserved and the logo was fully struck. The reverse side is etched with the name *Sandy Bauman*. Note the irregular choil cut.

Spacers on this knife are typical of mid to late WW II production, and the handle shape, butt cap, and wrist thong clip support 1943 manufacture.

We have read where Clarence Moore made alligator sheaths for some early Randall knives. Well, here is one and a beautiful example it is, obviously made to fit this knife right down to the last detail.

As a fighter this design was destined to be eclipsed by the Model 1. There is evidence that some were made after the all-purpose fighting knife and stilettos were incorporated into the line, but the commando faded from production by war's end.

Dick Raynor Collection

SPRINGFIELD FIGHTER WIDE BLADE

Varying blade grinds are not unusual on Springfield Fighters, but this one is wider than usual and is almost Model 14-like in appearance. Note the full blade and deep stamp. The clip point breaks more like a period Randall Model 1 than a Springfield and adds to the illusion. From the brass guard back, this knife more closely resembles the typical Larson-made knife. The guard is nicely shaped and is set off by three thick spacers, which appear to be red-brown-red forward, and thick red, thin brown at the butt cap. Although this stack is not unusual, it contrasts with the three medium-thick arrangement more commonly seen on many of the grinds attributed by the author to Northampton Cutlery Co. (See essay on the Springfield Fighters in *Randall Fighting Knives in Wartime*.)

The aluminum cap has the familiar tang nut, which protrudes about $1/4$ of an inch and is drilled for a wrist thong. This thong appears to be original to the knife, or at least period. The leather washer handle exhibits the usual contour and shape of these early fighters. For comparison see the following photo that illustrates the points mentioned above.

The Mosser-made sheath, original to the knife has been reinforced with a brass strip probably to prevent the mouth from being broken down by repeated sheathing. The snapped keeper strap fits snugly around the leather washer handle.

SPRINGFIELD FIGHTER

This Springfield Fighter appears to have escaped the War and use in general for that matter. Its owner was given the knife as a Boy Scout and with the exception of some personal hand polishing, put the knife away in his sock drawer, as it was too good to use. There it lay, untouched for many years. The blade is full and deeply stamped and without any sign of field use. The guard and handle shape is reminiscent of Larson's best efforts in reproducing a Randall-made fighter for the War effort and the quality is top notch. This spacer arrangement, thick red, medium white, medium blue (black) are found on these pieces with regularity.

The sheath is a practically unused Mosser with typical "loose stitching" using white thread. The open stone pocket flap reveals a contour, which begs the question whether the prototype sheath from which these were copied was a Clarence Moore, or a Moore copy of a Southern Saddlery. The white stone is labeled "Norton Abrasives, *Lilly White Washita*." Note the size of the throat rivets, which tend to vary. The snaps have been polished.

SPRINGFIELD FIGHTER SERIAL NUMBER ON SHEATH

The sheath says something about the person who owned this knife and whether there is any carry "documentation" or not seems to be a moot point. It was not uncommon practice to inscribe or scratch a service number into these sheaths and whether this knife was actually carried during combat is information unavailable to me. It was even a step further to go to the trouble to have a professional letter etching. Because of the original blade condition (as well as the condition of the sheath) my guess is that it may have been carried, it definitely was sharpened, but does not appear to have been used.

I rate this knife pretty high on the survivor level for a Springfield Fighter, due to the overall condition and high grade of workmanship in evidence here. We have previously discussed the various blade bevels, grinds and finish work and have photographed them in *Volume One*. This one belongs in the well-made class. The blade has some minor storage marks but exhibits the *original grind lines*. Additionally, the stamp is full and very deep at *Randall Made,* strong and clear at *SPFLD MASS*. Soldering is good and tight around the guard, which has achieved a beautiful patina, likely due to having been undisturbed over the years.

The spacer arrangement is representative of the period's better-crafted pieces, as is the handle shape. The leather washers are tight and the handle has been darkened, as has the sheath. The tang nut has oxidized, as most have over the years, but it is full and firm. I believe that the leather thong is period.

The sheath photographs nicely, as the darker tone has given it some depth. There are signs of carry: the stone pocket has been scuffed, the embossed lettering somewhat worn, and the sheath back smoothed a bit. The condition, however, is very good to excellent, with strong rivets, snaps and stitching. The pocket has not collapsed so that it must have carried the stone all these years. The discolored white stone is without a label, but period, and most likely original to the knife.

This piece presents an impressive image and there is evidence to support the belief that the Springfield Fighter was well represented in the Armed Forces of the United States during the Second World War and Korea.

MODEL 1-7 FIGHTER
MID-1940s

This fighter places us right on "the bubble" with respect to the WW II period. My feeling is that it most closely reflects the forging made somewhere in the middle of the decade, but later than the conspicuous blade shapes of the early WW II period. The top line is interesting as it shows a deep recess directly above the choil and an uneven blade back that lifts to a hump where the sharpened clip begins its angle to the tip. The clip measures 3¼ inches and the blade 7¼. This knife has seen no use and hasn't been sharpened; therefore the original grind lines are prominent. Sheath storage has marred the potentially "perfect" blade however. The brass guard also reflects even patina and the spacer arrangement is all medium thick, front and back. The butt cap is secured with a small brass nut and washer. It appears that the wrist thong is period leather and knives from the middle 1940s on would have a hole in the butt cap to attach it.

Heiser made the sheath and the stone pocket was "relieved" around the top edge in order to facilitate removal, although this one doesn't look used. The stone has its original paper label from Norton Abrasives still attached. This one was made in Troy, New York rather than Worcester, Massachusetts. Small rivets clutch the mouth of the sheath and a large rivet secures the handle keeper. The snaps have been affected by oxidation, but are secure and in working condition. The rear of the sheath is simply stamped with a 7, indicating blade length.

MID-1940s MODEL 1-7 FIGHTER
RUSSELL H. PALMER

This Model 1 fighter with seven-inch blade seems to be typical of the Randalls made during the mid-1940s. A gift from a WW II US Army Air Corps pilot to his father at about war's end, it undoubtedly represented the high compliment that the presentation of a well-made knife such as this conveys, as it mirrored the six-inch fighter carried by the son throughout the war.

This knife would see no such action and, as a result, retains its "period look" with the addition of a few storage marks and blade patina.

The angle of the photograph captures the distinctive bevels of the blade as well as the curve of the top bevel and the flat between them, which runs all the way to the tip. The blade back has a pronounced lift at the top of the clip and the "belly" is deep; all of which indicates an early grind. Note the forward spacer arrangement that shows a thin blue spacer in the center of the stack. The handle retains its cigar shape, but is a bit narrower at the neck and has more contour than the very early fighters (1942-1944).

The thong is the original leather attached at the shop. The left side carry Heiser sheath is in like new condition, with the logo snaps replacing the painted metal buttons of previous years. The stone depicted is original and retains its label.

Russell Palmer was a career Police Officer in the city of Detroit and the Ada County Sheriff's Department in Idaho. His son, Gordon, whose knife appears in the Carried Piece section, survived the war and continued to serve his country throughout a thirty-five year career.

LITTLE COMMANDO

Some knives are easier to identify than others are; this is one of the others. Early during WW II, Bo Randall built a "Commando" fighter; a knife, when in its development stages, had some unique fighting characteristics, not unlike the one in this photograph. The Classic Commando, as portrayed previously in this section, differs in some respects, but its overall similarity begs the question: "Is this one of those?"

There are differences, beginning with the blade length, which measures six inches, and the top clip that is beveled rather than sharpened. Then there's the shape of the guard, of three-quarter size and configuration. We know that Randall offered a "Hunter" model that became the "pilot" for the redesigned Model 3 after the War. However, even the Hunters as depicted in Gaddis and early Randall catalogs, were not ground like this. Perhaps the short-lived commando, made obsolete by the emerging Model 1, gave birth to a smaller, more versatile all-purpose field knife, while maintaining most of the design features. We may never know. In any event, it is convincing in appearance and with a sharpened top (bevel), would seem to offer the same fighting configuration as its bigger brother.

The sheath varies little from the larger commando scabbard; just a bit downsized in order to fit the knife dimensions. A very nice piece of work, whatever the intent.

George Torres Collection

1940s MODEL 5-6

This is not a Model 1, but it has the attitude of a "fighter" and makes a nice package for compact belt carry. The Model 5 was created from the Model 1 design by beveling the sharpened top, using a half-guard and modifying the handle to a "hunter" style. This one was made in the 1940s, probably late during the time when the Shop temporarily eliminated the tang nut. The red spacers in the front stack are thick and display a very thin black line running through the center. This feature in fiber spacers can be seen throughout the decade of the 1940s.

The overall condition of the knife and Heiser sheath and the small number of these "modified fighters" in circulation make knives such as this of special interest.

John Cheek Collection

EARLY 1950s MODEL 1-7

The nut/washer arrangement places this "original condition" seven-inch fighter somewhere in the first half of the 1950s. Medium thick spacers at the guard reappear about this time, but are most usually seen with a domed nut on the butt cap.

Note the light brown color of the leather washers, which do not appear to have been frequently handled. The blade has a deep choil, steep clip and its original polish, a well-preserved example of a fifty-year-old fighter.

Heiser made the sheath. Note the wide stone pocket (flap), which carries a two-tone gray.

EARLY 1950s MODEL 1-8 STAG

Stag has its proponents as a knife handle, and on an early 1950s Model 1-8, it is compelling. This particular stag (and the one on the stiletto following) was spared any handling and retains the original finish after all these years, as does the blade itself. We all have our favorites and mine is a fighter with an eight-inch blade from this period; stag, ivory or leather.

A customer option on some handles was a butt cap and finger grooves, but this knife shows stag from guard to pommel, held in place by a brass pin. When dating a knife, we look for help from the spacer arrangement. This one has a thick center spacer that is indicative of the time frame and a pinned handle is seen through the mid-1950s. Viewing the guard we notice the long oval shape as well as the soldering which is heavy and uneven.

If the original sheath is present as this one is, then we can reinforce our assessment through careful examination. This Heiser has a flare at the mouth, a wide stone pocket, and stitches way up on the flap, as well as some signs of the cutting tool on the rough side of the sheath back. Altogether it seems to confirm that this piece was made early in the 1950s.

MODEL 1-7 STAG WITH COMPASS HEISER SHEATH

The camera looks into the handle end in order to help us to better appreciate the stag of the day and show off the compass inserted into the butt; a rare option on a fifties fighter. This handle is pinned with finger grooves, all nicely done. The guard is nickel silver, which must have been quite popular during those times as we see a good deal of it. The seven-spacer stack had been standardized by the time that this knife was made.

The seven-inch blade is nicely ground, slim, but of thick stock measuring almost a full quarter-inch in width across the blade back. Note the depth of the choil.

Heiser made the sheath and it has painted metal snaps on both locations. This, and the wide stone pocket, point to the early fifties. The unusual markings on the back show two 1s over the logo and 1 over 7 underneath deeply stamped.

Dave Harmon Collection

EARLY 1950s MODEL 1-8 FINGER-GROOVED IVORY

We begin to see ivory appear during the late 1940s, and more frequently in the early 1950s when this knife was made. Eight-inch fighters were also becoming more common and this one has all the characteristics of a blade forged during that period. Unused, the blade shows the uneven bevels and hammer marks representative of the handcrafted knives of the day. Nickel silver was introduced about the same time as ivory (a customer option) and this fighter has both. Considered an upgrade, nickel silver created a different look than brass and also matched the butt cap.

The guard exhibits a longer lower quillon, which is often seen during this period and would be "standardized" a few years later to more or less equal proportions. The "shop" ivory has been finger-grooved, not a common choice during that time. Compare with early period fighters depicted in this volume. The front spacer stack is the usual seven, with a thick blue center spacer, and the rear arrangement has been filled out with a similar configuration, but substituting thick red for the front and rear spacer. This is most unusual, eye appealing and serves to stretch the handle. The aluminum butt cap has a brass washer and small steel hex nut.

One would expect to see an impressive sheath with this fighter and the light tan Heiser with "wide mouth" is indeed impressive. Snapped, the handle keeper fits snugly around the contours of the finger-grooved ivory. HH Heiser quality was always superior and this is reflected in the contour, stitching and finish of this sheath. Note the wide stone pocket flap, which corresponds with the length of the guard and is indicative of sheath construction during the early 1950s. The stone is a white Washita, period and original to the sheath.

1950s BRASSBACK FIGHTER HEISER SHEATH

"Brassbacks" are usually associated with Randall Bowies and with good reason, as the initial adornment of the brass strip was an innovation made on the Bowie models of the early 1950s. Someone liked the idea well enough to order this brass strip on a Model 1 all-purpose fighter and here it is!

Unlike the larger blades, many of 3/8-inch stock, this knife, in comparison, had little blade back to affix the brass. Gaddis writes that only one individual had the skill to accomplish the job. When we look closely we notice that the strip exactly follows the top line right through the thumb recess. It's careful work and doesn't appear to visually change the design features of the blade.

The rest of the knife closely resembles the mid-fifties style. Note the domed nut and spacer arrangements.

The sheath is a Heiser with brown logo snaps, stamped with the maker's logo and the model and blade length on the back.

The knife is the proud possession of collector John Cheek.

1950s MODEL 1-8 LEATHER

A refined guard and characteristically short handle set off the broad blade on this mid-1950s eight-inch fighter. Notice the deep choil cut and thumb notch just above the logo which, when stamped, rolled over the bevel. The Randall shop had returned to medium-wide spacers at the guard. The Heiser sheath is marked on the reverse side, 1 over 8, and the stone pocket flap is narrow, another sign of the period.

The handle keeper is un-riveted and is retained through a slot cut into the belt loop. Although rivets had disappeared by 1950, backstitching provided the necessary extra strength at the throat of the sheath. Brown opaque buttons are also typical of the period and continue through the life of Heiser sheaths, well into the 1960s.

1950s MODEL 1-8 COMMANDO STAG

The Model 1-8 depicted here can probably trace its origin to the late 1950s. This was a time when Vietnam was just beginning to get "Advisor" assistance and the Number One fighter was still a favorite of US servicemen. The handle on this knife has the swelled center "commando" shape that became popular on fighters earlier in the decade. This one is shaped from stag not leather, a carryover from its popularity during the Korean War. This serves to change the look of the knife and for those who prefer this style, it is a nice custom upgrade.

The sheath reveals "field expedience" dying and together with the diagonal keeper distinguishes this Heiser from other period sheaths. Thought to be of later production, there are many examples of this type of sheath design seen throughout the 1950s. Johnson adopted the diagonal keeper for all of his sheaths some years later.

The Green Beret depicted has the Special Forces enlisted crest attached and is dated 1962. The earliest berets were purchased from Germany and Canada until regulations and manufacturers' specs standardized this piece of uniform for authorized wear. This one was made in Canada. Needing no introduction, Special Forces elements made an early appearance in Southeast Asia and provided vital training and assistance to RVN staff, cadre and troops.

Peter Cuervo Collection

MODEL 1-7 LUGGED HILT

Swelled center (Model 2 style) handles on fighters gained in popularity during the early 1950s and must have retained appeal throughout the decade, although we seldom see them after that on leather-handled knives. This one is a seven-inch version and probably from the same period.

The blade on this knife is narrow and the photograph picks up the grind lines, which verify its original shape. Note the deep choil cut which persists into the 1960s when they then became shallow in comparison. The one unique feature is the lugged hilt, a carry over from the big Bowie models in the mid-1950s, and seldom seen on all-purpose fighting knives.

The sheath is a Heiser with brown logo snaps and diagonal keeper strap, dyed black by the owner, and the dye being removed from the stone pocket snap. All in all, this is a nice tight stitched sheath with the "lugs" fitting snugly over the throat and together with the knife, presents a compact carry package.

Gary Colpitts Collection

EARLY 1960s 8-INCH FIGHTER STAG

An additional ten years of knife making since the crafting of the similarly handled eight-inch knife of early 1950s vintage depicted earlier, produced this style of fighter. The Johnson brown button sheath original to this knife helps to place production about 1963. Handwork is still quite in evidence in the rippled blade.

Notice how the shallow choil and thumb recess appears to streamline the blade visually, when compared to 1950s fighters. Carbon steel still remained the choice of both Shop and customer during the early 1960s.

The stag on the handle is nicely shaped and finger-grooved for easy indexing. The guard is not as long as previous designs, just a fraction over $2\frac{1}{2}$ inches, compared to almost three inches on fighters from the previous decade.

The sheath has all of the design features of period Johnson production and has a two-tone gray stone in the pocket.

MODEL 1-8 STAG DOUBLE "SS" STAMP

Stag has its advocates and the handle material on this fighter has a nice drop that contributes to the overall appeal, as well as to positioning in the hand. The nickel silver guard and seven-spacer arrangement further enhance the knife. The finger grooves add another dimension to the handle. Although in unused condition, what contributes to its rarity is the "SS" stamped on the ricasso. By the time this fighter was crafted, (1964?) the demand for stainless steel had driven Randall to indicate it on the blade. Prior to this, Bo's partiality to his carbon tool steel was reflected in the small numbers of stainless blades manufactured, and stamping was probably considered unnecessary.

Notice the depth and misalignment of the "SS" which was really a single "S" double struck. It soon became evident that this was a time consuming and unscientific method and it was discontinued. The single "S" located low on the ricasso, and struck in the upright position, was the next in succession of stainless marks.

The double "SS" stamp has appeal and brings this early to mid-1960s knife to another level of collector interest. The sheath is a Randall waxed Johnson with brown logo snaps.

1960s MODEL 1-8 LOW "S" WALNUT

The chronology of the stainless steel stamping on Randall Knives is "double S", "low S", "separate S" and "logo S". The significance is the relatively short time that the first three stampings were utilized. As a result, dating is made easier, rarity is established, and collector appeal increases. Compare the shape of the blade with those of the late 1950s to early 1960s knives previously depicted.

This is an unused knife with many upgrades: scalloped collar, walnut escutcheoned swelled-center handle and coolie cap. The light tan sheath has all of the characteristics of a well-made Johnson with the two-tone gray stone still in its wrapper.

EARLY 1960s MODEL 1-7 UNMARKED LEATHER SHEATH

This fighter has been carried and shows normal field use. It is paired with what appears to be its original sheath — a Heiser look-alike. This pairing underscores the need for determining the age of a knife by examining the knife alone, as the sheath in this case is an unmarked copy.

Presented with two similar seven-inch "fighters" in section six, this knife suggests circa 1960 manufacture. The photograph in that section helps us to visualize it. Note the longer handle, shorter guard, domed nut, spacer arrangement and the reduced angle of the sharpened clip, all of which indicate early 1960s vintage.

Having dated the knife, we are better able to speculate about the sheath, the construction of which is of high quality and favors the style of a contemporary Heiser. We know that during that period, RMK was seeking a sheath maker. This one was obviously made by a skilled craftsman and notwithstanding the uneven trim on the stone pocket, displays careful machine stitching throughout. It also has brown buttons, which would have been provided to any potential supplier along with a prototype sheath to copy.

This sheath is unmarked, unlikely to be a Heiser, and possibly the work of an interested potential supplier that might include Maurice Johnson himself. There is no proof; therefore we call it the "missing link," as its owner, *collector Walter Rhyne*, refers to it.

Photographed with this knife is a wool ARVN Beret, belonging to a South Vietnam Airborne Ranger, reportedly KIA in 1967.

VIETNAM ERA MODEL 1-8 STAG FIGHTER

The Model 1 underwent some changes during the mid-1960s, upgrading the "old fighter" to then present-day standards. The changes made for a seemingly more combat sturdy all-purpose knife; a requirement no doubt brought on by the Vietnam War and the influences of new ideas and technology.

This knife carries some of these changes, which can be identified on the blade by the shallow choil and the addition of saw teeth as well as the guard, by its large size and extremely long length — $3\frac{1}{4}$ inches. There was also room for personal embellishments and the contoured stag handle and flanged cap and collar bear this out.

The sheath is a Johnson rough back of late 1960s vintage, photographed against a jacket sized patch commemorating South East Asia War Games, 1970-1971.

Ronnie Beckett Collection

MODEL 1-6 DELRIN HANDLE

Delrin is a plastic material introduced during the mid-1960s in an attempt to reproduce a "stabilized" ivory. However, as time has revealed, there is more to ivory than a pure white, flawless, unchecked surface. So this substance, which marked easily and didn't do well with heat, passed from the scene. In the meantime, it adorns handles on some interesting and well-crafted knives and in some cases, as it does in this, enhances the overall appearance.

A six-inch blade with saw-teeth is not a common configuration, but the blade length is practical and the teeth-altered shape has a certain appeal. Note the nickel silver guard that serves to tie the handle, blade and butt cap together.

The white stone that accompanies the sheath helps to date the knife and places it about 1970, when manmade handle material began to replace shop supplied natural substances on Randall made knives.

Peter Cuervo Collection

Chapter Two
FIGHTING STILETTOS

The oldest style of personal protection knife influencing Western civilization has been the double-edged type. It's a stabbing knife and a design that is difficult to improve upon. European culture saw the knife evolve across national borders in a relatively similar style and evidently the principal differences were the ethnic names denoting origin, i.e. English dagger, Scottish dirk and Italian stiletto. It was the latter name that Bo Randall selected for his Model 2 in the early 1940s.

This section features some of these knives and the "standardized" design that Randall adopted and periodically modified in order to satisfy the requirements of the times. It's likely that the blade design will be around forever, notwithstanding the truly American Bowie style replicated in the Model 1, 12 and 14.

The introductory photograph for this section depicts a knife from the early 1950s, my choice to represent the array of blade shapes, lengths, and handle materials available during the past sixty years of Randall Fighting Stiletto production.

1943 MODEL 2-8 DOUBLE-STAMPED MOORE SHEATH

A Randall stamp on both sides of a single blade is uncommon, but double stamping appears on this knife. The camera side shows the logo "way out there," two inches from the guard. The reverse side stamp is one inch forward of the hilt, just below the median and the blade is also name etched above the stamp.

The fighting stiletto was introduced shortly after the fighter and didn't receive a great deal of publicity. Its reason for being was due to the influence of the BC stiletto on the thousands of US troops working with their British Commonwealth counterparts.

The Randall innovations found on the Model 2 included hand-forged steel of high grade and a more stable and suitable blade for all-purpose field use; the stiletto not normally associated with anything other than stealth "man work."

It's doubtful that this design accounted for even 10% of the total estimated (5000+) knives handcrafted for our servicemen during wartime production. Additionally, it appears that few of those stilettos were in blade lengths exceeding seven inches. This is one of those knives with a blade measuring eight inches. The wrist thong clip or link fashioned from brass, in this case indicates early manufacture, probably 1943.

The blade shape, guard and handle are indicative of the "original design" which is very functional in appearance, yet dagger-like in style.

Accompanying the knife is its handcrafted Moore sheath, a slim profile leather scabbard that almost hugs the contour of the blade. Note the absence of rivets at the throat, the long stone pocket and scalloped flap. The snaps on this sheath are representative of those apparently available to Moore during this period.

Direct ties to military use have been lost, but information provided indicates that the knife was the property of a US Navy member who served during WW II.

1950s MODEL 2-7 PINNED STAG

Sometimes a knife photographs best with just its sheath. At first glance, it has all the look of a 1940s "fighting stiletto," but on closer examination, we see that it was most likely produced during 1950-1951 and the sheath bears this out. The spacer configuration and the early dark stag are reminiscent of earlier work, but this arrangement can be seen on many examples of early fifties knives. The pinned stag handle is long and has a little flair at the end, which fits the little finger nicely. Note the blade grind, which has taken on a more streamlined shape and the stamp, which appears on the ricasso.

The sheath has lost its keeper strap, but the wide stone pocket, lack of throat and keeper rivets and metal snap, are each indicative of this period.

John Cheek Collection

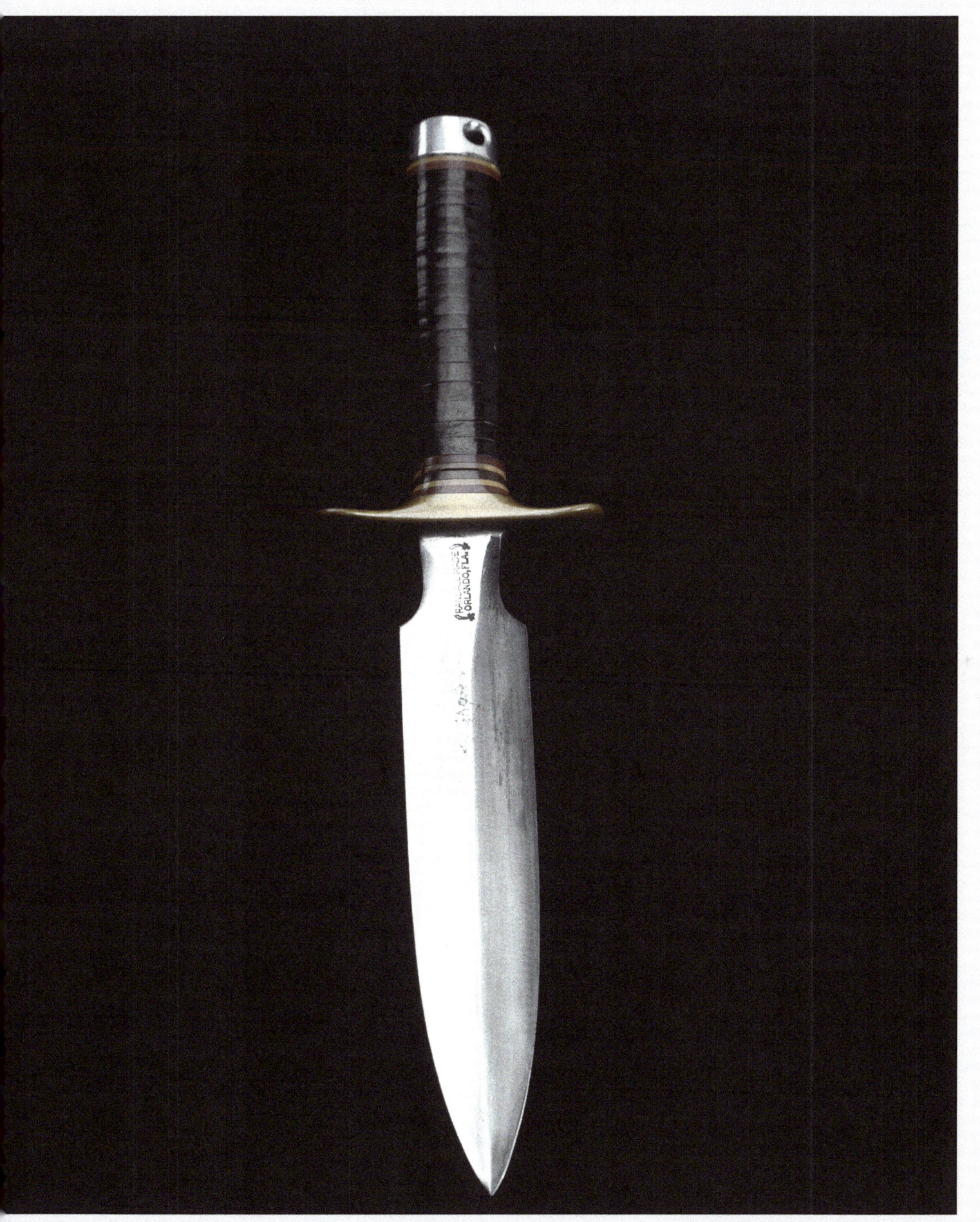

1940s FIGHTING STILETTO

This is a nicely shaped knife, probably mid-1940s. The blade measures 6-5/8 inches, the fractions being common during a time when the exact blade length of handcrafted knives was not a priority. Note the large stamp on the ricasso, no longer forward under the median, as were the early 1940s models. The brass guard has a nice patina and the handle still retains thick washers and "cigar" shape, with a short contoured butt cap, drilled for a wrist thong. A nut washer secures the cap. The spacer arrangement at the guard is 5-thick, while the three spacers at the rear include a metal spacer at the end.

The original sheath is no longer with the knife, but if it were, we might expect to see a Heiser, with either metal or plastic logo snaps, and a white stone in the pocket.

John Cheek Collection

1950s MODEL 2-8 – IVORY

As previously noted, ivory has its proponents and, as a handle material, a good deal of visual appeal if not practicality. After introduction as a customer option in the late 1940s, it is seen to appear on both fighters and stilettos more frequently. This one shows the wide center spacer of the very early 1950(s) arrangements, as well as a pinned handle. Nickel silver was another option and is frequently seen on upscale models of all types.

The blade measures eight inches and carries a small stamp on the ricasso. Note its very characteristic design reflecting production of this period.

The Heiser sheath, with handle keeper and brown logo snaps, carries a terra cotta colored stone with fishhook sharpening groove. This type is found circa 1950 in many sheaths of various models.

Dick Raynor Collection

1950 FIGHTING STILETTO 9-INCH BLADE

A knife ceases to be a knife and becomes something else when it exceeds normal standards. This "stiletto" has an inch on the standard variation, but still retains its knife-like characteristics. While lengthening the blade, similar treatment was accorded the handle, partly for balance and probably for aesthetics as well.

The blade shape remains true to the grind of the day, as is the location and size of the stamp. The reader will take notice of the front spacer stack and nut/washer arrangement at the butt cap.

It is quite likely that this was a customer special order knife, as Randall did not offer a catalog version in a length exceeding eight inches. The sheath seems to confirm the obvious when we begin looking for a maker's logo. *Who made this sheath?*

The answer lies not on the reverse side, where no maker's mark exists, but on the obverse. If we concentrate here we might observe the following: close contouring, burnished edges and no overlapped stitching at the throat. Contrast this with a wide stone pocket stitched without split edges at the base and a large pocket flap without contouring. Let the reader determine as we present this sheath with comparison models in another section of this book.

Dick Raynor Collection

STAG MODEL 2-8
EARLY 1950s

The Model 2-8 depicted is a "mate" of the fighter similarly dressed and previously photographed in Section One. They were kept together in a small collection purchased new by the original owner and then carefully preserved. It is doubtful that the sheath(s) were ever on a belt. We can find the same period characteristics on the stiletto that we identified on the number one. Blade style, choil cut, long oval guard and thick center spacer: Identical.

As matched pairs are uncommon, these knives are depicted as a set further on in this book.

1950s MODEL 2-7 PINNED STAG – HEISER

As a handle material stag came before stacked leather washers on Randall knives; here's one good reason why. Although this fighting stiletto was probably produced during the first half of the 1950s, the stag appears earlier and has more of a 1940s look about it. Note the rich, dark course pigment and the size of the pin. Although used in the beginning on his first knives, stag didn't appear on fighting knives until well after WW II, and probably as late as 1948. So a knife like this takes a visual step backward in time.

The blade measures seven inches, an ideal length for a sheath knife designed for fighting — not too long, nor too short. Logo stamping had shifted location from the blade "flat" to the ricasso. The limited space required use of a small stamp introduced for early blades of small dimensions. The blade also shows its original bright finish (polish); while the knife itself is a reflection of innovative stiletto handcrafting a full half-century after it was produced.

HH Heiser had become the sole supplier for Randall made knives by the time that this sheath was made. The time of Denver snaps and painted buttons had passed and brown opaque buttons would be standard until the introduction of the Johnson roughback, a full decade later. Notice the wide stone pocket flap on this close fitting sheath. This one is typical of the design and the craftsmanship of the time.

MODEL 2-6 IVORY MODIFIED SHEATH

This photograph depicts a beautifully crafted stiletto with six-inch blade, nickel silver guard and pinned ivory handle. Knives of this type, featuring blades of this length, are not common, especially during the 1950s when this was made. Note the nicely shaped swelled center handle which is held in place by a brass pin. The nickel silver guard was considered an upgrade.

The sheath accompanying the knife is interesting, to say the least. The belt slits are standard on the model "B", while the remainder of the sheath is clearly a model "A" type. The handle keeper has been added and is riveted through the center of the Heiser logo. This package has been carried some and used a little. The blade retains its full but slim profile and has some signs of hand cleaning.

Together, knife and sheath make a secure but accessible field combination, as well as an impressive addition to any collection.

Dick Raynor Collection

STAG FIGHTING STILETTO EARLY 1960s

At first look this blade design appears to favor 1950s vintage. Note the deep choil cuts and the narrow ricasso. Despite this, the standard sized stamp was used. This stiletto belongs to a set, paired with a fighter depicted earlier, and replicates the size of the guard and length of the stag handle. However, finger grooves that appear on the Model 1 are absent, as they were seldom cut into stiletto handles as the swelled center commando style was more popular.

The sheath features the wide-mouth style of earlier stiletto design and carries the logo snaps of the Johnson brown button period.

DOUBLE "SS" MODEL 2-8
EBONY – EARLY 1960s

This knife, which appeared in *Randall Fighting Knives in Wartime*, deserves another look in the author's view. Ebony was not the most durable of handle material, but did lend itself to shaping, and the flat sides of the handle permitted quick indexing of the "stiletto" blade; a not so easy task when round.

We identify with the early stainless steel blade as well, indicated by the "SS" (stamped twice) on the ricasso. This doesn't leave much doubt as to the approximate date of crafting. Always a favorite with military men, the Randall Model 2 has been dressed with various handles styles throughout the years, but the blades have a commonality that stand the test of time.

The sheath is a black (dyed) version of the Johnson roughback, which by this time, 1964, featured chrome plated snaps rather than brown buttons.

Photographed with the knife is a U. S. Navy Seal Team badge.

1960s MODEL 2-8 LEATHER

The Model 2s, as well as the 1s, underwent a decisive change during the late 1960s when a broad blade and handle were introduced: That was after this knife was crafted. In this "fighting stiletto" we observe a medium-wide blade with narrow choils, which was representative of the early to mid-1960s. The blade is carbon, which continued to be the steel of choice until late in the decade, when the impact of service in Southeast Asia made stainless more practical and appealing for use in the jungles of Vietnam.

Dating requires some understanding of the many aspects of a knife. Reliance only on spacers and sheaths is superficial and, as often as not, will lead to confusion. Note the handle contour on this knife. The swelled center is less thick than 1950s knives and the length not only compliments the blade shape, but also represents a change in style that begins to be seen in the early 1960s and which will disappear shortly after this piece was made.

The brass butt cap and guard show nice even patina and seem to bring the handle together visually. The spacers on this knife are characteristic of the entire decade and therefore further illustrate the pitfall of over-reliance on these arrangements for accurate dating. (Medium-thick red; thin white; medium-thick blue; thin white; medium-thick red.)

Notice the sheath shape and quality of the leather. It is well made with a narrow profile that compliments the shape of the knife. This sheath was made by Johnson and is referred to as a roughback because the unfinished side faces out to the rear of the sheath. The stone is a two-part gray, which was used from the mid to late 1950s until replaced by a return to white (in some cases solid gray) about 1968. The later stone(s) were interchanged, depending upon the supplier's inventory.

MODEL 2-8
WIDE COMMANDO HANDLE

The width of the blade and the narrow choils stand in contrast with the wide contoured "commando" style handle on this fighting stiletto. If not a customer request, then the "shop man" reflected back on earlier times when shaping the leather. Notice the aluminum cap that extends the taper to the butt and gives the impression of a 1940s style handle.

Production was probably about 1970 and the steel is stainless, marked with a "logo-s." The sheath is a Johnson roughback with tight stitching and there is a soft Arkansas stone in the pouch. The knife/sheath combination represents the late Vietnam period of the early 1970s when the war was nearing conclusion. Although not appearing to have been carried in any theater of operations, collectors identify with the period, which has a heavy attraction in the field of militaria.

Walter Rhyne Collection

MODEL 24 GUARDIAN
THE SMALLEST STILETTO

Most Randall fighting knives are associated with our military services, but not this one. Inspired and then developed as a result of a customer's suggestion and introduced for concealed carry, this hide-away knife with stiletto-style four-inch blade was created with law enforcement in mind.

Like the Model 18 before it, a customer with a special requirement did the initial planning. Once in the development stage, the Shop did the rest and the result is this very functional knife/sheath combination.

Notice the serrations at the base of the blade, which permitted forefinger and thumb to move forward of the guard engaging these blade notches for cut and slash use. The interesting "fishtail" shape of the micarta butt was designed to provide a place for the little finger to rest when thrusting.

The sheath itself is a study in innovation and affords multiple carry positions for this "maximum concealment" knife.

Chapter Three
FULL TANG KNIVES OF THE VIETNAM ERA

The format of this book does not follow the three major wars exclusively, as does *Randall Fighting Knives in Wartime*. Recognition is given in this section to the several models that were developed during the span of years when we sent troops to Southeast Asia, as these knives are inseparable from that conflict. With some duplication inevitable, the variations in the fighting knives from this time frame make a strong case for further examination in detail. The early years during the Vietnam buildup saw the introduction of the Tenite-handled Models 14, 15, and 16, which have strongly left their imprint on the period. This is also true to a similar degree of the same models handled in brown micarta. These knives, and the hollow-handled survival knives that followed soon after, form the essence of this section.

MODEL 14-7-1/2 TENITE ORLANDO BLADE

Here is an example of an early "Attack" model with extended tang and "green" handle. The blade on this knife measures 7½ inches and is stamped *Orlando Fla*. Note the *slider* attached to the wrist thong, a feature utilized on some of the early models, as seen in the contemporary catalog(s). These "14s", more than any other Randall models, seem to epitomize the Vietnam era in the minds of servicemen and collectors alike.

The sheath, marked on the back *Randall made Knives, Orlando Fla.* and stamped with a 14 over the logo and 7½ beneath, was made by Maurice Johnson. The lift-the-dot fastener, a concession to security and first introduced by Heiser, (or Moore) retains the keeper, replacing the brown button snaps that we see on the stone pocket flap. This is a well made sheath, tightly stitched and riveted to prevent separation should the stitches rot or break loose.

The split back construction simplified placement of a "frog" by stitching and riveting a rectangular piece of leather, approximately 2½ inches by 5½ inches to the sheath back, thereby forming a belt loop for waist carry. This two-part construction would later give way to one solid piece of shaped leather.

The final product, dyed brown and waxed, is close fitting and holds the knife snugly in place. Note the leather ties on the belt "frog," adjusted for handle security. A similar tie (leg) is coiled at the tip. The rivets are all of the same type, peened over on the back. This would change when the nickel-plated snaps replaced the "canteen snaps" on the keeper strap with large harness rivets at the throat. The stone is a two-part gray by Norton.

When viewed together, this carry package is impressive and was understandably the popular choice of so many US ground troops.

BROWN MICARTA MODEL 14-7½

The focus of my attention when I first looked at this knife was on the "wood-grain" texture of the handle material, which we call brown micarta. Cut with the grain, this handle actually looks like wood and undoubtedly represents an early lot of the material, which appears to vary on some later knives. The flat sides of the handle appear like "slabs" and add to this illusion. Eventually the micarta was cut across the grain, which produced a totally different (current) visual effect.

This knife is of the prototype design with extended tang. Brown micarta followed green tenite, but there is no easily identifiable date of change, rather a trial and error transition period that saw the use of several color tones of this material, as well as different methods to affix it to the knives.

As it turned out, micarta did replace tenite and eventually became a permanent standard handle material on all full-tang Model 14s, but not this brown variety. Its appearance for a brief time in the early 1960s marks the time when the knife itself was redesigned to eliminate the extended tang and incorporate a wrist thong hole in the handle proper.

Incidentally, this was a modification recommended by the USMC equipment board some ten years prior in their evaluation of the test knives submitted for combat use by RMK and others.

The flat guard on this knife, although not as long as some depicted earlier, reveals the "squared-off" ends — a consistently early shape. The handwork on the guard stands out as well. The blades on Model 14s were either Orlando or Solingen-made and this one is the former, with a strong stamp and shallow finger cutout forward of the guard.

Another transitional point is the design of the sheath. The Johnson canteen-snap, which made a brief appearance on some Model 14 tenites, has been replaced by a brown button (snap) on the keeper, as well as on the stone pocket. The construction is split-back with the use of rivets. The sheath shows some contouring and is very well made, which is typical of these early Heiser look-a-likes by the new sheath maker, Maurice Johnson. The maker's logo is on the belt loop, front side. Where Heiser used their own logo on these sheaths, Johnson chose to incorporate "Randall Made Knives" onto his work.

Stanley Kanakaris Collection

BROWN MICARTA MODEL 14-7½

The brown micarta Model 14 on the previous page has an extended tang with the wrist thong hole drilled through the extension. This knife, with like handle material, was made with the handle covering the full length of the tang and the thong hole drilled through the handle. That this change in design took place during a period of handle transition makes accurate dating of a piece like this more probable (mid-1960s).

The first micarta handles were brown and we can read in Gaddis that some of the early material was problematic. Micarta continued to be experimental, which accounts for some of the *slight* variations occasionally visible in the replacement lots of the procured material. I use the word "slight" with emphasis, as all of the real stuff is unmistakable and shouldn't be confused with the early black variety that was to come later.

The method for attaching the handle to the tang followed the initial process used on the experimental USMC knives on plastic and tenite handles; that is, they were bolted on through the tang.

Tenite proved to be susceptible to the heat and humidity of Southeast Asia and this was to eventually require a replacement handle of "indestructible" material. In the process, epoxy was introduced, even on tenite, before that green plastic was discontinued entirely.

Not a great many knives appear to have been constructed during this brief, experimental time period, which helps to explain the variations incorporated on late tenite and transitional brown micarta handles. This circumstance makes brown micarta (as well as epoxied tenites) very collectible.

The knife photographed here has a long guard (3 1/8 inches), an early grind and the Orlando blade shows multiple ripples from the forging process (hammer marks), which will not appear on machine forged and pre-ground blades made in Germany. They are not always present on Orlando blades either, depending on polishing procedures used at the time. It does spell out handcrafting however, the signs of which recur throughout the 1960s and then disappear altogether, as techniques become more refined.

The sheath is s splitback with large throat rivets. The stitching favors the earliest Johnson type(s) and is beautifully finished.

MODEL 15-5½ TENITE JOHNSON CANTEEN SNAP

Folks often overlook the fact that the "Airman" is a little fighter and this one seems to emphasize the point. An early knife, to be sure, with its radical top line, with hump and steep clip, small stamp on the blade, its short shallow choil, the narrow oval guard, long extended tang and finally, the slider on the wrist thong.

Compact even in a "C" sheath, these then "new" tenite-handled Model 15s offered what amounted to a strengthened Model 1 blade with a full tang and a handle calculated to withstand the elements. What's more, it's knife-like and it feels good in the hand. The superiority of this original design is obvious.

Maurice Johnson made the sheath and it has the "lift-the-dot" fastener commonly referred to as a canteen snap. It also has the original leather ties and is riveted like the Heiser that served as a prototype. The back is deeply stamped with a 15 over 5½, as was done on the early Johnson sheaths. This one was dyed brown by the original owner and nicely done.

MODEL 15-5½ EXTENDED TANG

A great many Model 15 knives saw hard service during Vietnam; this one escaped it. As typical of the tenite 15s (when compared to the later micarta-handled knives), the blade is narrow with a small guard and smaller gripping surface. With its full tang, it probably doesn't need more bulk and seems more knife-like up against a 1970s "Airman."

The survival rate for many of the knives of this design can be attributed to the specialists who ordered them. As the name implied, many of the 15s went to aircrew personnel, as did the shorter Model 18s in 5½-inch length.

Not as popular as the "Attack" model tenite, the overall size and suitability for their intended purposes made this an enduring favorite.

The sheath is a Johnson brown button with large rivets at the throat. Construction of the back is two-part, which creates a seam at the bottom where joined; hence the name "split-back". These well-made sheaths would be hard tested in Southeast Asia and they stood the test. A beret with Ranger tab and jump wings provides the backdrop for this depiction.

MODEL 15-5½ NAME ETCHED

Every Randall knife is forged by hand, ground, fitted and polished, to ensure a high standard of workmanship. Therefore, no two knives of the same model are exactly alike. This Model 15, blade etched *Soubier*, is distinctive for this reason, even without the name on the blade. Adding to the subtle differences is the accompanying sheath, which features the same careful attention to detail and often reflects the maker's art in the way that it way constructed.

This sheath shows brown buttons on both snaps, two large rivets at the throat, three small rivets at the tip and two at the top of the belt loop. The color is dark tan probably due in part to the limited use it has seen. The reverse side reveals a rough, almost unfinished side out on the top section, which is joined just below by the large rivets. Leather ties accompanied these sheaths and the one visible in the photo is adjusted for handle security.

The knife and sheath are photographed against the background cloth of a US Army field utility shirt with stitched jump wings and combat infantryman's badge.

MODEL 15-5½ EPOXIED TENITE

Many collectors will seek the earlier extended tang tenites and sometimes overlook the later version with handle epoxied, rather than bolted in place. This variation reflects a step along the way toward standardizing the "Airman" and was not made in great numbers. The reason for the change reflects an attempt to stabilize the material, which characteristically shrunk and sometimes warped away from the tang. The modification did not completely eliminate the problem however and the subsequent introduction of micarta made further modifications unnecessary.

Therefore, we can usually identify the period that this method was used (late in the life of tenite on RMK) and also concede that there were fewer of them.

This knife has a blade marked "Solingen" and is made from carbon steel. If stainless was used then we might observe a double "SS" or lower "S" on the ricasso, as this represents a comparable time frame. Notice the color variation in the "green" when compared with tenite handles bolted in place and also the handle length, which is extended in order to accommodate the wrist thong hole at the same location (as the extended tang models) without lengthening the tang itself. The guard still retains the small size consistent with early models.

The sheath is a typically well-constructed Johnson "split-back" with large harness rivets at the throat. The stone in the pocket is two-tone gray. Depicted along with the knife is a set of "Tiger Stripe" camouflage field utilities, which show an interesting vertical pattern, possibly of French influence. They are unlabeled and hand marked with an initial and name.

MODEL 16-7 TENITE DIVER

We featured another extended tang Diver handled in tenite in *Randall Fighting Knives*. This is not the same piece. Randall knives are handcrafted and therefore will show some differences in the same model from knife to knife.

This blade is narrow, which is somewhat characteristic of the period during this early development stage of Model 16s. *(See the comparison photograph in the Sets section of this book.)*

Initial examination of the knife would lead one to believe that the steel is carbon, as it is unstamped. However, this period predates stainless steel stamping and both steels were available, carbon being the option. Stainless steel went unmarked until the demand required stamping and this model, introduced during 1958, was not frequently ordered until later in the 1960s. I would also add that up until this time, Mr. Randall reportedly favored carbon steel for his knives. Vietnam was to change this. In any event, the unblemished condition on this fifty-year-old full tang knife would suggest stainless steel.

The waxed Johnson sheath carries a nickel-plated steel snap and the knife previously referenced has a brown button. These sheath snaps may have been interchangeable during this time frame, as the former was replaced by the steel snap. Other differences include the location of model and blade length stamping.

These extended tang Divers in tenite are the rarest of similarly handled full-tang knives, as far fewer were made and, by the time that the Vietnam War had heated up, tenite was no longer available, having been replaced by micarta. The tab depicted is a First Cav. LRRP.

ASTRO – *SPACE ODYSSEY*

Few Randall knives had the pre-catalog notoriety of the "Astronaut" knife, or the genuine and purposeful collaboration of such highly trained specialists who would eventually carry them in space. In spite of the legacy of the "Astro," the Model 17 would never compete with the other "Nam era models" in popularity, albeit not intended for that purpose.

From the beginning, a special creation for an historic *Space Odyssey*, we were to witness all seven Mercury astronauts carry their Randalls into space and eventually into the Smithsonian Museum.

The special design features of the knife were then unique; a sharpened drop point blade for safely cutting through space suit material, large guard to facilitate use with gloves and a hollowed out tang for carrying survival items in the handle cavity.

Notwithstanding its overwhelming approval by astronauts going into space, it was denied an opportunity to fill another role by the introduction of a "hollow-handled tube" knife with saw-teeth, intended for earth rather than space use. Regardless, the type still remains a testimonial to an innovative design that served a purpose far exceeding its popularity when eventually offered to the public.

Depicted here is an Astro with early grind, handled in brown micarta. The reverse side of the blade is shop-etched *1965* and shows the slim profile and handwork of the forger(s) grinder and polisher of the day. A comparison with a later Model 17 is provided in Section Six of this book.

EARLY 1960s ASTRO BROWN MICARTA HANDLE

The handle on this early "Astro" is a distinctive reddish-brown in color. There is speculation that this knife was one of several that were made up for project Mercury support personnel sometime later than the original knives sent to the astronauts. This could explain the color variation. The initial knives, photographs of which have been widely circulated, reveal the micarta to be a light brown in color. The brown micarta that was used on many subsequent full-tang models following this was darker brown with "wood grain-like" texture visible in the material. The latter can be seen on several knives photographed in this publication, as well as in *Randall Fighting Knives in Wartime*. Interesting and unique, it presents the possibility that there are others out there with similar material.

The brown snaps on this sheath would date the knife circa 1963 and this confirms that it is early production. The unused Johnson is stamped 15 over $5^1/_2$ on the rear and the construction is split back. Leather ties are usual for this period, but they do not always accompany the sheath.

Peter Cuervo Collection

MODEL 18-7½ "ATTACK-SURVIVAL" FULL TANG KNIFE

Early "Attack-Survival" models have these things in common: a large "squared" guard, distinctive blade shape, saw-teeth, a hollow handle with tang extended within, and a rubber "crutch-tip" that serves to secure the end of the tube. This one has a compass set into the end of the rubber cap, a nice addition for a survival knife. As the design did not as yet permit attaching a wrist thong to the guard, the cap has a grooved out recess for that purpose. This was most probably an upgrade, replacing the cotter pin briefly used earlier and would give way to the drilled guard soon to follow.

The full, well-preserved blade is stamped *Orlando*, and shows a less radically shaped top line than German-made Solingen blades of the same period. The sheath is a split back with customary large rivets at the throat. The *Randall Made* stamp, identifying Johnson as the maker, is visible on the upper portion of the sheath.

Peter Cuervo Collection

18-7½ CRUTCH-TIP WITH HANDLE WRAP

The nylon cord handle wrapping on this "tube" was probably original and provides a practical, if not eye appealing gripping surface. Additional application includes using the line for field survival purposes. The rubber crutch-tip serves to safeguard the hollow handle contents, in this case somewhat restricted by a tang extending one-half way, that is filled with epoxy right to the end of the tang.

Later use of epoxy would be limited to the base of the handle, thereby providing additional space on either side of the tang for small items such as water purification tablets, matches, and fishhooks.

The blade on this knife is etched *Solingen*, along with an "s" for stainless. The saw teeth, characteristic of this model are "medium" in size, beginning just behind the bevel line and running almost to the logo. Note the absence of a hump on the top line where the "teeth" appear to run in almost a straight line. This is in contrast to the earlier grind on the full tang knives where the blade back exhibits more contour.

The sheath is typical of the period and is of one-piece construction, reinforced with small copper rivets. The stone pocket holds a white Washita marked *soft Arkansas*. These stones were interchanged with solid grays, as dictated by their availability from their provider, Norton Company of Worcester, Massachusetts.

MODEL 18-7½ SEPARATE "S" BLACK SHEATH

The Attack-Survival model was available in either Orlando hand forged or Solingen (Germany) machine forged and ground blades. The choice was simplified during the Vietnam War due to the reduced waiting period (6-8 weeks) for the finished knife using the latter blade. Many of these went to Southeast Asia and were used.

The Orlando bladed crutch-tip required more time to craft, and that period, perhaps as long as a year, could have coincided with a completed tour of duty. This might explain some of these very popular pieces not showing signs of use.

This knife has the distinctive large full blade of the Orlando type, is deeply stamped with a separate "S," shows fine "teeth," and has its original polish. Identifiable features include an offset in the angle of the guard and a pinched tube that contains a half-tang with epoxy at the base. Construction was probably late 1960s.

Note the black sheath. This one was dyed at the Shop and has the smooth side out on the back, making it easier to hold the dye. The punched holes in the belt loop and the absence of black dye at the throat are also indicators that this was a professional application.

18-7½ SOLINGEN CARBON BLADE

Unlike the preceding photograph, this "Attack-Survival" knife shows an unwrapped tube pinched at its base. Squeezing the handle permitted alignment with the rectangular shape of the guard. Later modifications included rounding the hilt to better conform to the circumference of the tube. The blade itself, logo-etched as Solingen's were, features large saw teeth. The sheath is identical to the one on the previous page and is representative of Johnson's work during the late 1960s. There is a two-tone gray stone in the pocket, which reflects the overlap in stone types that occurred around these times and reveals why exact dating by stone alone is a shortsighted business.

Survival cards were issued by the government to help educate the American fighting man about the various plants, reptiles and insects that posed a threat in the Vietnam jungle and countryside. Photos and descriptions enabled identification and suggested treatment when contact was made.

MODEL 18-7½ EXPERIMENTAL TUBE

Crutch-tips predated screw-caps and necessitated a squeezed tube in order to accommodate the relatively narrow rectangular guard adopted from the Model 14 "Attack," a knife that gave the "Attack-Survival" some of its original design features; namely the blade grind and full tang.

Early introductory models had a capped tube to safeguard the contents of the hollow handle and a "crutch-tip" was used for this purpose. Initial attempts to design a suitable screw cap were unsuccessful but eventually the process allowed for it and this knife appears to be one of the very early designs featuring a brass cap rather than a rubber tip.

The specific changes required to implement this design are seen on the Model 18 photographed here. Note the 1/8-inch thick tube walls, which are deeply threaded to accommodate the length of the heavy knurled brass screw cap (which appears to have been filed by hand); the walls of which match the thickness of the tube. The unique brass center ring, designed for a wrist thong is soldered on from the inside base of the cap. This differed greatly from what was to become the final arrangement on this model. With respect to practicality, the soft brass ring could be flattened during use and this is probably one of the reasons that it was not included in the final design. (Dominique Beaucant, in *RKS Newsletter #25*, wrote about this unique feature in his column *Collectors Choice*.)

A rounded reduced tang is visible part way up the tube and is soldered in place without the use of epoxy. These design features ushered in a change in the shape and contour of the guard, which is more rounded at the ends. Note the initials in the brass, which appear to have been Shop etched.

The wide Orlando blade stamped with a separate "S" features saw teeth. *The weight of this knife is 19 ounces!*

The sheath is a Johnson *splitback* that closely accommodates the knife in fit. The throat and keeper strap marks and impressions indicate that it has long accompanied this early and unusual experimental hollow-handled survival knife.

MODEL 18-5½ CRUTCH-TIP ORLANDO BLADE

The mid to late 1960s are associated with the Solingen bladed knives partly due to their availability on a faster time frame. The crutch-tips of the era with the shorter 5½-inch German-made blades appear to be large in contrast with the knives forged and ground at the Randall Shop during this time. Part of the reason is the top line of the former that, even with saw teeth, followed the contour of the "hump." Here is an Orlando blade that stands in sharp contrast and is slim and refined in comparison. Note the almost straight top line in spite of the teeth and the almost refined design of the blade. The small guard helps to set it off while tying it in with the hollow handle. This is nice work and the size and shape of the knife helps to create the image of a believable small survival carry knife.

The sheath is a well-made Johnson splitback with large rivets. The original ties have been braided, as this knife was never carried. The pocket holds the original two-tone gray stone.

Photographed with the knife is a personalized "sea bag," highlighted by the hand painted figure of a "Geisha" in full costume.

MID-1960s ORLANDO BLADE CRUTCH-TIP

This crutch-tip has a very early blade grind and saw teeth configuration. The guard is small and lacking drilled thong holes and the tube is long measuring a full five inches. The handle itself has a very thin wall, approximately 1/32 of an inch in thickness with the tang measuring just over three inches in length from the base of the tube. There is no epoxy.

Old fishing line serves as a handle wrap and the contents of the storage area, squeezed down around the tang, are displayed in the photograph. Note the crutch-tip with grooved recess for a thong.

Ownership of this knife during the 1960s is attributed to Cpl. Robert Koly, US Army, Vietnam, 1966-1970.

The sheath is a Johnson split-back with large rivets at the throat and a two-part gray stone in the pocket.

Dick Raynor Collection

Chapter Four
CARRIED KNIVES

The essence of this section is the presentation of the carried piece and, where appropriate, to confirm and document its use in a wartime theater of operations. The latter is not always possible, as the thread of ownership is often broken. However, in large measure, a knife used by a member of the Armed Forces of the United States often reflects some signs of military use in the field and for the purposes of this book will merit inclusion, documentation notwithstanding.

We often categorize a "carried knife" by the appearance alone and that is usually quite acceptable. Handle wraps, missing stone pockets, belt attachments, leg and arm ties, blade and sheath etchings, special order riveted sheaths, all point to the obvious; we shouldn't overlook the obvious. Documentation refers to the discovery of specific references linking the owner and the knife and placing the two together in a period that is both historical and interesting to the collector. This circumstance adds to the credibility of the knife for those whose interest runs to military or wartime use. There is a place for both in our collections.

Unfortunately, many knives have been taken out of their original condition by over-zealous enthusiasts and in spite of their proclaimed interest in a period of conflict, ultimately eliminate any evidence of it. Hand cleaning and "Shop" attention are remedies that may at times be necessary and even desirable. On the other hand, removing years of patina, storage and handling marks, signs of field sharpening, minor pit scars, and the etched name from a blade in order to replicate its final polished state when new, only serves to sever the connection that we are trying to preserve — a historical link to a past event.

By normal definition of the term, "beaters" are excluded in this publication. They reflect poorly on the user, if not unnecessarily on the blade, and therefore give an incomplete and misleading picture of the knives when presented. Honest care and reasonable use are the criteria that we have used relative to the condition of knives photographed in *Randall Military Models*.

Finally, and most importantly, I would like to help introduce the reader to the lure of the "used" knife, designed and crafted for our servicemen of all branches, in the condition in which it was most probably carried while in service.

MODEL 2-7½ WITH FULLER

In *Fighting Knives in Wartime*, we have seen another Stiletto with a fuller, but they are exceedingly rare. This knife is a bit more refined than the first, with the *blood groove* running almost the entire length of the blade beginning just forward of the choil-cut and ending almost at the tip. The Randall logo is right up there against the groove edge of the fuller, two inches forward of the guard, and is deeply stamped. At some point, years ago, the blade was cleaned at the Shop and retains its full ¼-inch thickness. The spacers are typical for a knife made during this period (1943), and the leather washers are almost equal width on the oval handle (4 7/8 inches). The overall look is long and slender and the knife has smooth lines and beauty of form and proportion as a result of its symmetry. Note the shape of the butt cap, which is gently tapered to coincide with the shape of the handle. A steel wrist thong link is held in place by a small brass hex nut.

The sheath is clearly early and represents a Southern Saddlery throat riveted model. Sometimes confused with Moore sheaths, I believe this example is typical of their work. It exhibits large brass snaps, wider stitching, a more generous contour and quality not equaling Clarence Moore's. Note the sculptured shape of the stone pocket, which may be the result of copying a prototype (Moore), sent by RMK. The reverse side is unmarked. The stone pocket holds an early Norton stone — unlikely the original.

The history of this blade is as interesting as the knife itself. The original owner, Christopher Myland, purchased the fuller in 1943 from a gun store in Orlando while he was training as an officer cadet in the USAAF. The knife accompanied him throughout the war and was part of his equipment during numerous flights in the Caribbean where he served. Interestingly enough, Lt. Myland volunteered for infantry duty and was schooled in 1945, but the War ended before he could see ground action. As a member of the Reserve, Cpl. Myland was called once again to active duty when the Korean conflict began and he served for two years in a combat zone, his Randall Made Model 2 on his side. Below are some disclosures from his personal letters regarding his Randall knife.

"There was hardly a day that went by that someone didn't ask to see my Randall knife. (Korean service) I was always glad, and sort of proud to do so. By the way, the knife had a leather thong loop attached to the top of the handle that you put your hand through before grasping the handle. If you released the knife it swung back into your hand."

". . . I mentioned Charles because he could never keep track of his can opener. I kept mine on my dog tag chain and he was always using my knife to hack open his rations."

"I had to cut one commie Korean to get his attention. I'm not denigrating this knife but I firmly believe a bullet from a distance is much easier to live with."

"After 5 battle stars the knife and I rotated to Japan and then home. Nice. On Cape Cod I fished for 18 years commercially on my own boat and used the trusty knife on sharks, they have touch skin."

WW II 7½" FIGHTER WITH HEISER SHEATH

Unlike the decades that followed, most of the fighters made during WW II went to US servicemen and many in an overseas Theater. This one is an early forties example with thick red spacers at the guard and a wrist thong link at the other end that secures its original leather tie. The butt cap, narrow and rounded at the end, is a style that was phased out by the time a hole was drilled for the thong.

The knife is used, but the blade has been well cared for. The top bevel is distinct, but the blade has a "flat-sided" look with little indication of a ricasso and that is typical of these very early WW II fighters. This one measures 7½ inches in length, more typical in these early knives than measurements to the exact inch and the stamp is out there, two inches from the guard.

The guard shows a different color than later brass. Note the neatly block-etched initials and last name, which is untraceable at this time.

The handle is typically short, measuring 4½ inches from the front of the guard to the end. The sheath is an early Heiser, with an "8" stamped under the logo. This is a well-constructed sheath, revealing close contouring and tight stitching, a keeper placed high on the loop and a very long tab on the stone pocket flap *and it is without throat rivets*. The snaps have large brass buttons, peened over on the underside. The original stone, photographed here, has been broken.

One battle that every Marine has fought is the "battle of green-side out," referencing the green (and brown) reverse side of camouflage utilities and referring to "changing the word" which happens from time to time in the Corps. Suitable period background material is hard to find and this "paramarine" camouflage jacket is just plain scarce. Official photos of the war show both sides being worn "out," usually brown on the beaches and green in the jungle. Note the slash pockets, which were unique to the "Airborne Marines" and contribute to collector appeal.

WW II 8" FIGHTER ETCHED USMC SOUTHERN SADDLERY

The previously depicted WW II fighter shared the same background material, but this one is showing the green side of the "paramarine" camouflage utility jacket.

The knife is a "fighter" with a 7¾-inch blade that has obviously been carried and used and we have photographed the reverse side to focus on the name etching: *Charles F. Luedtke U.S.M.C.* The blade retains the early grind, with a "flat-sided" look, short choil and little ricasso. Note the deep patina of the brass and the shape of the quillons. During the early 1940s, we are accustomed to spacer thickness as represented at the butt cap. The front arrangement has two very thin reds, two thin whites and a medium blue spacer, not at all common during WW II. The handle is short and measures 4½ inches from the front of the guard to the end of the butt cap. The wrist thong is formed by bending a 1½-inch shaped steel clip and fastening it to the butt cap with the tang nut.

Accompanying the knife is an excellent example of a Southern Saddlery sheath that carries its original stone. These sheaths were unmarked and identifying them has led to some confusion, as they appear to closely resemble the Mosser-made sheaths supplied with Springfield Fighters. The latter was probably a copy of this Southern Saddlery style, and goes a long way to support the assertion that one of these sheaths accompanied the prototype knife sent to Larsen in Springfield, Massachusetts. In any event it is a well-preserved specimen and is depicted again, with comments in the sheath section of this book.

Dick Raynor Collection

WW II MODEL 2-7 FIGHTING STILETTO ETCHED "COOK"

This "Fighting Stiletto" made an appearance in *Randall Fighting Knives*, and is presented again in this section as it represents a more or less typical example of a WW II carried piece, notwithstanding the lack of specific documentation. Showing the reverse side helps to tell the story, as the blade is etched and the name is scratched into the sheath along with a regular Army serial number. This "field expediency" is typical of the personal modifications that servicemen sometimes scribe on their equipment during wartime. The knife shows signs of field use, as does the sheath, but both exhibit the care that preserved them some sixty years after the close of hostilities.

WORLD WAR II FIGHTER 10" BLADE

Who is to define the dimensions of a fighting knife? In this case and at least one other, (*RFK*, page 27) it was a USAAF pilot who decided to order and carry this remarkable example of a knife, designed to cut both ways! Exhibiting all of the characteristics of early production, the blade is etched with the date 12/1/43, which coincides with the return to the US of the then Captain Larry Leith, 8th Air Force Europe. The knife blade measures ten inches with a sharpened top edge of just over seven inches from the tip. The blade sides are ground flat, as are the knives of this period, with little ricasso and a deep choil. Note the stamp location. The spacers are 5 thick (mid-late 1940s standard) and the handle has little contouring from front to back.

The total weight of this knife is sixteen ounces, two ounces greater than the bolo featured in *Randall Fighting Knives*, and has a similar user-friendly feel; weight forward but responsive in the hand. Moore's work is in evidence in the sheath, which shows typically careful detail in fit and finish.

The owner's military service is well documented. Prior to the December 1, 1943 date on the blade, Lieutenant, then Captain Leith, served in the 8th Air Force as a night fighter pilot and the theater-made insignia commemorates this period of his wartime service. Subsequent duties were varied and included testing and training assignments in the US. Major Leith was discharged in 1946 and became a member of the Air Force Reserve.

Dick Raynor Collection

WW II 6" FIGHTER
GORDON PALMER, USAAC

Six-inch bladed "fighters" were not as common during WW II as the seven-inch and to a lesser extent, the eight. However, the size was a good fit for a pilot or air crewmen, long before the introduction of a knife created for their particular use.

This knife, with its radically angled top line, reflecting the influence from the earliest fighter, (Zacharias-Randall) and further accentuated by the short length of the blade, has all of the characteristics of Bo Randall's first fighting knives. Note the deep sweep of the cutting edge from choil to tip. The thick brass guard is the type usually seen on WW II knives. Typical of the period, the handle is full and somewhat oval with an interesting spacer arrangement at the thin butt cap.

A clip or link of bent steel served as a thong hole and was secured to the butt cap. The original thong is still in place.

The sheath is a marked *Heiser* with a "6" stamped on the front. This is another example of these early 1940s sheaths without rivets at the throat. The original stone with label is in the pocket.

The pilot who carried this six-inch fighter was Lt. Gordon Palmer. Entering the USAAC during 1942, he trained as a signalman in Orlando where he purchased the knife. His assignment with the newly formed 20th Air Force brought him to Tinian in the Marianas and then the Philippines where he and his squadron were part of the 6th Bomber group. Lt. Palmer flew B-29 "Flying Fortresses" during the closing months of the war in an operation that ultimately destroyed the Japanese war machine.

Gordon Palmer continued his service through the end of the war and then decided to make the Air Force his career, retiring in 1965 with the rank of Lt. Colonel. Impressed with the knife that he carried, he ordered a similar "fighter" for his father and that knife was delivered at war's end. (Section One, Palmer Model 1-7.)

Depicted with the Randall Fighter is a theater-made patch of the 20th, his wing insignia, dog tag, and a photo against the background of a B-29 with "nose" art.

WORLD WAR II FIGHTER
THE RAID AT CABANATUAN

Forward elements of the 6th Army led General MacArthur's liberation of the Philippines in a first strike at Luzon. The sixth Ranger battalion was selected to conduct an insurgency into enemy-held territory in order to free American prisoners known to be held by the Japanese since their capture at Bataan and Corregidor. Because they feared the prisoners would be put to death when the invasion began, a handpicked group of 100 Rangers, specially trained for this type of operation, conducted a raid at Cabanatuan. On January 30, 1945 skillful preparation and execution put the Rangers and their Filipino scouts within striking distance of their objective, a camp that held several hundred POWS.

The attack on the compound was carried out with complete surprise and accounted for more then 400 enemy dead. The Rangers freed weakened prisoners, transporting them on ox carts brought for that purpose and then fought their way back to US held territory with only a handful of casualties. It was a "classic" operation, using the Ranger team(s) as they had been trained and one of the most " . . . daring of the missions accomplished by men from this battalion in the Philippines."

Leading one of the teams was Lt. William J. O'Connell, whose men struck at the main gate and then cleared the open area in the camp of all Japanese. During the withdrawal, this team set up a roadblock to engage and delay enemy reinforcements on the way to the camp. Throughout this operation, Lt. O'Connell carried the knife depicted here. His ID card and Ranger Bn. tab are shown against a silk map that was issued and carried by men who participated in this theater.

The life of this knife did not end with the conclusion of the war, but was passed on to his son Paul who, while a member of the U.S. Armies 82nd Airborne, carried it in his pack on more than thirty jumps and used it extensively in the field.

The knife has a blade that measures $7\frac{1}{2}$ inches and has a wrist thong hole in the butt cap. It was probably crafted during mid to late 1944 and sent to the owner in theater. His comments reflect that other Randall knives were received in the battalion at the same time. The sheath accompanying the knife is a period replacement and bears the initials W.J.O.C.

Paul O'Connell Collection

MID-1940s MODEL 1-6
NAME ETCHED "HADWIN"

The hump on the top line appears accentuated by the relatively short length of the blade. Not common during the WW II period, this six-inch blade is name etched to a US Army officer who served between 1941 and 1947 in the Asian-Pacific Theater. His service number appears under his name on the blade. Apparently crafted during the mid-1940s, this fighter was probably ordered and sent to the owner in his theater of operations.

Note the shape of the guard and the "bronze" tone of the brass. This and other mid-1940s fighters were butt-cap drilled for a leather thong after the folded brass link, fashioned for that purpose, had been replaced. The handle shape was changing as well. Notice too, the narrow "neck" behind the spacer stack and the thick blue (rather than medium-wide) center spacer.

With the knife out of the sheath, the oval Heiser logo can be seen just beneath the handle keeper. Field expediency is apparent in the removed pocket, although the imprint of the stone suggests that the modification took place after it had seen some field use. The keeper strap retains the original rivet and metal stamp, while small rivets reinforce the throat. Some knives just look right with *equipment* and this six-inch fighter makes a nice compact carry package for combat field use.

Tankers are forced to work in confined areas, which impacts on the weapons that they select. A highly regarded favorite during WW II was the Thompson Sub-Machine Gun and the choice for a carrying case was this canvas type that could be hung up on the interior bulkhead out the way. The well-constructed zipper case depicted here is marked accordingly.

WORLD WAR II FIGHTER US ARMY AIR CORPS

Bob King enlisted in the US Army Air Corps in September 1942. Soon after, he was selected for pilot training and attended various qualifying programs until he earned his wings in early 1944. Subsequent assignments included Instructor School in Texas where he flew gunnery missions in twin-engine craft. He picked up his first crew in California flying B-24's in the Fourth Air Force.

The Fourth was activated in 1941 and, as a component of the Western Defense Command, initially had responsibility for the protection of the Pacific coast. As the threat diminished, it concentrated on training aircrews for combat operations. Its contribution in flight preparation for bomber, reconnaissance, and fighter missions in war theaters was significant.

It was during this time in early 1945, while flying in a training command, that Bob ordered and received his Randall Fighter. The $25.00 price was considered high, but the knife found its way into his survival gear and was frequently carried in his boot while flying missions from the West Coast. As Bob recalls, "Pilots all carried knives to extricate themselves from a downed craft or to cut parachute lines in the event of a bail out," and he was never without his.

Bob King served in the American theater throughout the war, with much of his time in a training role. He was discharged in 1946 and remained in the Air Force Reserve until 1958.

The knife depicted here with a photograph of the young pilot is an eight-inch Fighter. The reverse side of the blade shows the name etching. The more or less exact dating of delivery (early 1945) provides us with a verifiable example of knife design during this time frame. The blade is 1/16 short of a full eight inches and it shows a more refined style that earlier designs. The handle on this knife is five inches long. Note the "necking" down at the front spacers, which are standardized at five medium-thick. The wrist thong hole has been drilled through the butt cap.

Heiser made the sheath, which is stamped on the rear with a number "8" under the logo. There are metal rivets at the throat and metal snaps on the pouch and keeper. The handle keeper rivet is made from brass (or copper).

Courtesy of Robert E. King

WORLD WAR II 8" FIGHTER US ARMY

Following his older brother into the Air Corps in 1945, David attended basic training and was then assigned to a Military Police command. Shortly after, he received an unexpected "gift" from his brother and became the second family member to carry a Randall Model 1 during his abbreviated tour of duty with the Army Air Corps. Bob King had been so impressed with his knife that he immediately ordered one "just like it" for David King. The turn around time was just as fast and it was delivered in a few weeks. There is little more information about service time, but we know that David used this knife as a sportsman in the field during later years. The knife is almost identical in dimensions to brother Bob's fighter and the two are presented together in the "Sets" section for comparison purposes.

This Model 1 has been well cared for. The blade is full, but hand cleaned and the handle- washer-spacer configuration is fully intact.

Courtesy of Robert E. King, Jr.

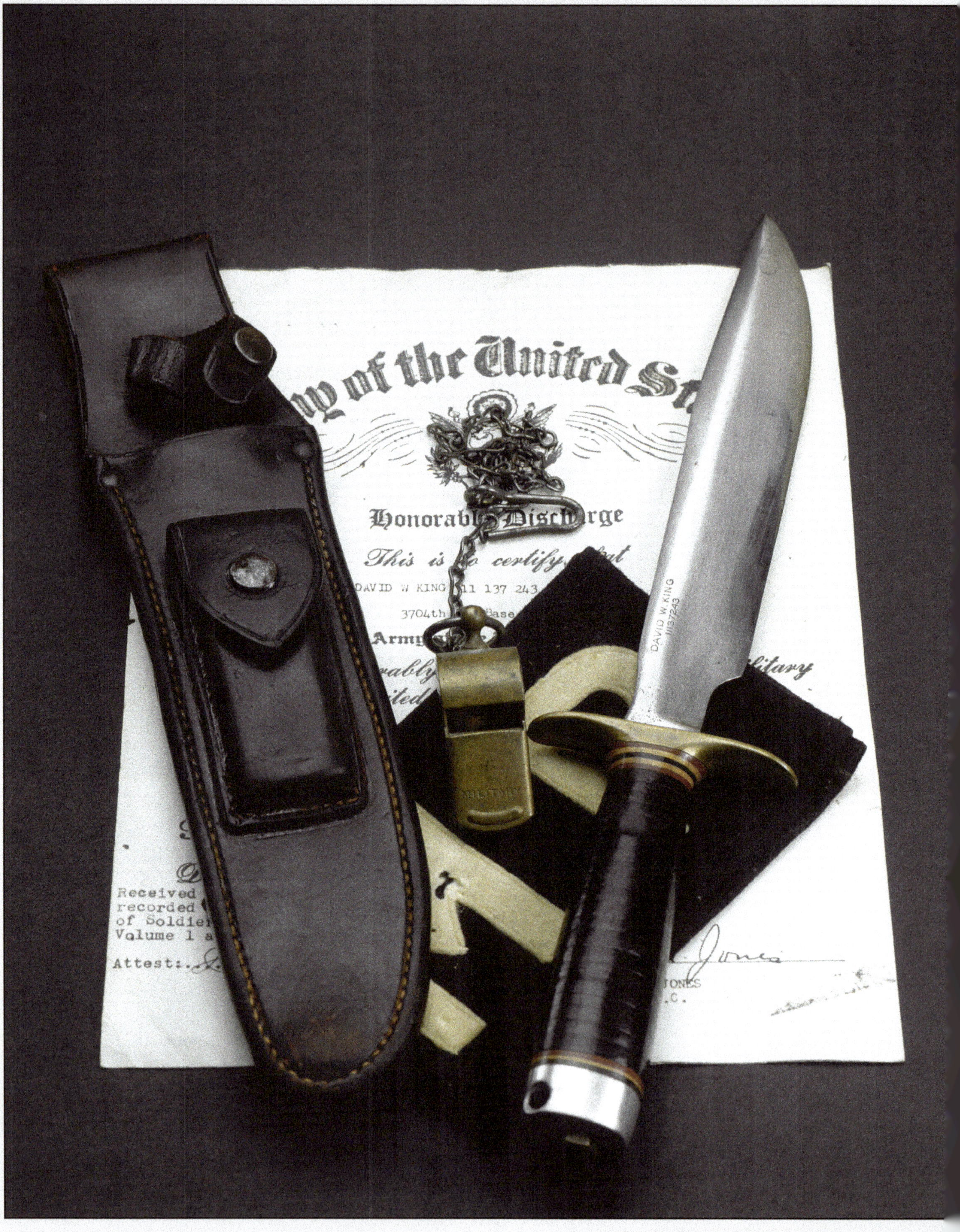

SALTWATER FISHING KNIFE
WW II UDT OPERATIONS

Long before introducing the Model 16, Mr. Randall had designed a true saltwater diving knife, one of which is photographed here. The knife is interesting, but so was the man who used it. A pioneer in spear fishing and skin-diving in general, Hal Messinger was an underwater angler of some reputation before entering the US Navy during WW II.

Subsequently he was elevated to a new position that put him in command of all combined forces of Underwater Demolition Teams (UDT). The organization was created through the influence of both the President of the United States and the British Prime Minister and Messinger's appointment was made on the recommendation of the OSS.

As a Naval officer, he organized, trained and developed the UDT's, which led to their successful operations in clearing enemy waters on invasion shores. During his service, Captain Messinger developed procedures used to pick up SEAL teams from a moving boat.

Hal Messinger carried the knife depicted during the war, but any reference to how and where it was used has been lost in time. Its unique design is devised from forging a $3/4$-inch bar that was hammered and then ground to shape out of one solid bar of stainless steel. The result was a rustproof knife that held an edge and was ideally suited to the type of work it was designed for.

John Cheek Collection

EARLY 1950s MODEL 1-7 KOREAN ERA

The spacer configuration at the guard is a rather precise indication of period, more so them other fiber arrangements of the 1950s. The thick center blue in this medium-thick/thin configuration was introduced very early in the decade and was replaced by the 3 medium-thick/2 thin arrangement so familiar later on. This was sandwiched around a return to the 1940s standard stack of 5 medium-thick during the mid to late 1950s. Other indicators include the washer and nut on the butt cap, handle shape, and, to a lesser degree, the narrow blade grind (blade length is $6^{3}/_{4}$ inches.). Note the choil, which is long, and shows the deeper cut that was used from roughly 1950 up to the brown button Johnson period.

Adding the sheath to the picture serves to reinforce the supposition, with its wide stone pocket and thick keeper strap. The stone is a white Washita, which was replaced by a two-tone gray Norton by mid-decade.

Seven-inch blades don't have the "stretch" of the eight-inch version and sometimes look a little stubby. This one is slim enough in profile to maintain a streamlined look while keeping its configuration for effective use as an all-purpose fighter.

All in all, this is a practical and efficient example of the early 1950s Model 1 produced at the height of the Korean War (1950-1953).

MODEL 1-8 – COMMANDO HANDLE KOREAN WAR

If there is a consistently recognizable fighter configuration from the Korean War era, it is the Model 1 with commando handle. This came about due to the increased popularity of the "fighting stiletto" that incorporated a swelled center contour for gripping. About the time that this knife was delivered in late 1950, this handle shape was available on Model 1 knives and caught on.

The blade on this fighter measures exactly eight inches and reflects the more or less "standardized" blade design of the 1950s; a more refined grind than the knives of the previous decade. There are signs of the age, however, in the use of solder, type of brass, spacer arrangement, and handle, which measures five inches. The latter would be reduced to a shorter length and not reappear in this extended length again until the early 1960s *(brown button Johnson period)*.

The sheath for this fighter has a flared throat, again typical of very early 1950s production. The maker's mark is stamped in a long oval on the back of the belt loop, "HEISER over DENVER". The stone is white.

Entering the USMC in 1949, Guy Paul Lockhart ordered this knife and received it prior to his tour of duty in Korea. His DD-214 lists his combat awards, which include the Korean Medal with 2 stars and the Presidential Unit Citation with one battle star. Other records of his service are partially displayed in this photograph, which includes a small flag neatly folded with his papers.

George Torres Collection

KOREAN ERA COMMANDO HANDLE FIGHTER

This Korean War fighter is typical of the early 1950s and the most recognized design associated with that era. All of the hallmarks are visible in this knife, beginning with the Model 2-type handle. Note the five thick spacers at the guard, which is small in relation to those of the previous decade. The nut/washer arrangement at the butt cap was to disappear in favor of a one-piece domed nut by mid-decade. Due to its utilitarian purpose, just like the previous war, many of these knives were used — some hard. This example saw service, but shows good care. According to the owner, it also saw service during Vietnam.

The sheath, a Heiser with diagonal keeper strap, was modified by stitching on a leather shank, which extended the length from belt to keeper by several inches. This was reportedly done by the 6' 8" soldier who carried it. This combat field expediency is the type of personal modification that helps to qualify an undocumented knife for consideration as a carried piece.

Ronnie Beckett Collection

LATE 1940s MODEL 2-7 RIVETED SHEATH "RIGHT OF PASSAGE"

Depicted in this photo is a well-used Model 2-7 with small stamp and thick center spacer in the 5-spacer configuration. The Heiser sheath is of late 1940s vintage, with rivets at the throat and a "transitional" snap arrangement of brown button keeper and painted metal snap on the pocket flap. This reflects the change from painted snaps of the late 1940s back to the brown logo button, which would eventually replace them on both keeper and stone pocket sometime during the 1950s.

The pocket carries a white stone.

This knife was carried in Vietnam and reportedly handed down through four succeeding Company commanders as the "symbol of authority" for that organization over a four to five year period.

Beginning in 1965, when the 1st Cavalry Division began operations in Vietnam, and extending into 1971 when they pulled out, this knife saw continuous use in the field. The last owner carried it home with him.

Depicted with the knife is his uniform shirt with in-country patch, boonie hat with rank insignia, and belt.

Walter Vedock Collection

1950s MODEL 2-7
"COURAGE ISN'T WRITTEN ABOUT...."

We have commented elsewhere on knives carried during successive wars. This is one of those knives. Made during the early days of Korea when the Model 2 was gaining in popularity, it found its way to Vietnam with the same soldier some years later.

The flag, bearing a brief description of a fight against NVA or Viet Cong, describes a victory that relates to much killing of the enemy and is dated 1963, a period of heavy commitment to the US Military Advisor program. The medals and Special Forces badge were the personal property of the owner, *H. Gordon Frost*, and his name is etched on the blade and on the back of the sheath. Note the long oval Heiser stamping and thick center spacer, both of which help to date the manufacture of this seven-inch "fighting stiletto" as very early 1950s.

The distinctive feature of the knife is the buffalo hide, stretched and sewn over the handle and sheath. This was definitely an in-country innovation and suggests the lengths that the Advisor went to adapt to his environment. The back of the sheath faces the camera in order to display the inscription: *"Courage isn't written about, or talked of . . . it is done,"* a hardcore epitaph from a dedicated warrior.

George Torres Collection

TENITE "ATTACK" MOORE SHEATH

Moore sheaths accompanied the prototype "Attack" knives depicted in Bob Gaddis book. The photograph on page 143 of *Randall Made Knives* shows a Model 14 and 15 pair, both with an affixed Eagle, Globe and Anchor (EGA), just like the sheath in this photo. Additionally, the fourteenth printing of the Randall catalog also shows an early Moore "C" type sheath with rivets but without the EGA.

This example makes probable the assertion that this knife and sheath combination was put together in the mid-1950s; therefore dating back to the earliest Model 14s made.

Note the blade shape, especially the abrupt drop of the sharpened clip. The knife has been carried and used and the "green handle" shows the effects as well as the blade. Unfortunately, its history has been passed on only by word of mouth.

It would follow that Moore got the original work for early 14s due to the new design and the close proximity to the shop. This example, and early Heiser production in Model "C" sheaths, makes for an interesting comparison. Its excellent state of preservation (45+ years) contributes to the importance of this leather knife scabbard.

Ronnie Beckett Collection

GUARD-ETCHED MODEL 14 HEISER CANTEEN SNAP

This green handled knife is a typical example of the carried knife. Circumventing the necessity of supporting documents, the knife (and sheath) tells the story and captures the viewer's attention with its unique visual characteristics. Little more need be said after seeing the etching on the rim of the brass guard.

This period piece, blade etched as well, was produced during 1959 after a visit to the Randall shop and a special "hand-fitting" session with Bo himself. Delivery took place shortly after and the knife accompanied a young Airman on several tours in Vietnam. It remained in his possession until after retirement some twenty years later.

The sheath, in conjunction with the knife, bears some of the distinctive signs attributed to field use referred to in the section introduction, namely the attached hanger for web gear that is affixed to the sheath by a riveted leather piece on the back.

Heiser made a tight fitting sheath for this knife, somewhat narrower than the standard riveted sheaths that were to follow.

Knife and sheath are in the collection of Ronnie Beckett.

TENITE MODEL 14
SPECIAL FORCES AIRBORNE

The canteen snap had a brief tenure before Johnson replaced it with a brown snap. This was done during 1963 when the sheath and knife photographed here accompanied SP4 Charles Ash to Vietnam, where he served in Special Forces, 1st Group (Airborne) for a seven-month tour of duty. Assigned to B-320 as a radio operator, records indicate that he was entitled to hostile fire pay for the month of November 1963, for activity in and around Da Nang. Other missions extended Ash's engagement activity through the end of 1963. His commendations included the Vietnam Service Medal with 2 stars, Vietnam Campaign ribbon with device and Vietnam Gallantry Cross with unit citation.

A likeness of the soldier is depicted in a photograph wearing his Model 14, which is carried on the right side, and the outline of the handle and tang can be identified, small as it appears in the image. The knife has seen field use as evidenced by its blade and sheath condition and both have been well maintained. Notice the hanger on the Johnson sheath.

This Randall knife and a very complete set of official records were provided to the present owner, military knife *collector Donald Anderson*.

BROWN MICARTA 14-7½
HUFNAGLE USMC

It's routine to photograph a knife with the logo side up, but name etching and other distinguishing marks are struck on the reverse side. This Solingen Model 14, which has seen service in Vietnam, first appeared in *Randall Fighting Knives* where the blade is depicted in the obverse. We have photographed a full-length image for inclusion in the Carried Knife section of this book, which reveals the blade etching. The serial number helps to date the time of enlistment for the Marine as early 1960s. The knife with brown micarta handle was probably produced about 1964-65. The grain in the handle shows well in the photo and is representative of true brown and not black micarta with a brown tone. The blade is carbon steel, made prior to the increased demand for stainless steel that was soon to follow.

Note that saw teeth are rare on a Model 14 from this period and not offered as an option until the eighteenth printing of the catalog in 1967. According to Gaddis, they were occasionally requested and Bo reportedly made exceptions for military personnel. There are twenty-eight "teeth" cut into this blade.

Definitely a carried piece, further documentation was not available to the author. Another good reason to preserve the blade etching on these knives.

BROWN MICARTA MODEL 15 "AIRMAN" HOAGLAND

Brown micarta is collectible, if not always easily recognizable. Knowledgeable collectors have sometimes been misled into believing that some "brownish" (black micarta) handles were in fact brown and the discovery that they weren't has led to uncertainty about the material, to say the least. There is no mistaking this one. Initially, the color gets our attention and this is a deep reddish brown, but in finality it's the grain, running vertically in the handle, that provides conclusive identification. The wood-like grain that shows up in the photo is typical and the color is correct as well. Note the filled screw hole in the center of the handle; another indication of the period that brown micarta was used (although not exclusively). As this was a transitional material, early replacement black micarta handles were affixed to the tang in the same manner and showed filled screw holes until the procedure was discontinued.

This Model 15 shows signs of carry and use. Further, it is name etched to *George A. Hoagland*, who served for twelve years in the regular Army and died in Vietnam on a combat mission. According to the documentation, the 1st Cav. had requested project Delta reconnaissance in the An Lao Valley during Operation MASHER and B-52 Delta landed at Bon Son and inserted recondo teams who were engaged in action by VC units fighting in their own terrain.

Hoagland was reportedly killed in the encounter and Project Delta would later record this as their worst disaster during 1965. The knife was later recovered by a team member and returned to the family of the deceased.

Vietnam veteran and military knife collector, *Peter Cuervo*, took the photograph depicting a section of the Vietnam Wall inscribed with the name of *George A. Hoagland*.

MODEL 16-7 BROWN MICARTA ROYAL CANADIAN AIR FORCE

The previously depicted "Diver" in green tenite predates this knife. Handle materials on this and other full-tang models were selected for indestructibility during field use. Tenite was durable, but warped and shrunk after exposure in humid climates. The search for a replacement for tenite lead to micarta and the brown variety was the first step along the way. Because it wasn't the final step, we observe an early and rare collectable variant.

For a brief period then, brown micarta adorned the full-tangs and this is one of those knives. The handle on this micarta Model 16 is epoxied and the use of bolts had been discontinued, leaving no filled screw holes to mar the micarta. This is a very good example of the reddish-brown layered resin with its distinctive wood grain-like composition. A very short time later, perhaps less than a year, black replaced brown and became the standard for all future full-tang models.

The blade on this Diver is ground in a distinctive spear point shape, which is a very functional style and perhaps would have been carried in theater to a greater degree if a Solingen blade option had been available. It was not. A six to eight week waiting period was a great incentive for servicemen en route to Southeast Asia.

The knife is featured in this section due to the blade etching, which identifies it as having been owned by a member of the Royal Canadian Air Force. The obverse side has the Randall trademark stamp without an "S". Obviously a custom order, the sheath is an "A" type with stone pocket and without model or blade stampings on the back. It is also close fitting and would have made a nice combat carry package for pilot or aircrew.

The knife is photographed against an image of the Arvo Canada CF-105 Arrow interceptor prototype.

MODEL 18-7½ USMC SNIPER

Every Marine is a rifleman; that's the credo and it has built a strong foundation for marksmanship in the Corps. In France, the 5th and 6th Marines were the most decorated Regiments in WW I and caught the Hun's attention at distances of 1000 yards with bolt action Springfield's. In those days, and during the following World War, sniping was not highly regarded in the military, nor was it supported in special training programs.

Contemporary modern warfare has seen the role of the sniper universally accepted and the level of proficiency raised to a high degree. Sniper training in the USMC was spawned by the Marksmanship Training Unit through peacetime rifle competition and then formalized into Sniper School in order to create combat effectiveness.

Vietnam saw new standards met, with respect to sniper proficiency, and out of that war came the most recognizable name in the hierarchy of the profession: Carlos Hathcock. But he was not alone. Many Marines entered the field as snipers and served with distinction. The knife depicted here belonged to such a man and his name is etched on the blade, and it's been used some. Unfortunately, its history does not accompany the knife. On the obverse side, the blade is stamped Solingen with an "s" and stainless is etched across the ricasso. The guard is of mammoth length (3 5/8"), is rectangular and offset to the lower side with a full 1½-inch extension below the pinched tube. The sheath accompanying the knife is a Johnson riveted with one-piece construction on the back. Note that there are twenty-four "teeth" cut into the blade.

Bob Tronolone Collection

MODEL 18-7½
ONE HUNDRED MISSIONS

In 1967, Captain Carlson, then assigned to Shaw AFB in South Carolina and scheduled for a tour in Southeast Asia, ordered and received the knife photographed here. It is interesting to note that the Air Force had provided him with a jackknife that he felt was insufficient for survival purposes. Subsequent duty in Vietnam included flying in B-66C's as an Electronic Warfare Officer attached to 41st TEWS, where Carlson carried his "Attack-Survival" knife on 140 missions, 111 in North Vietnam. His comment, "If you have ever seen the low jungle in SEA you would understand why a knife like this is essential," could probably be attributed to many in similar situations when selecting a knife such as this.

The life of the knife continued throughout the career of the now retired Lt. Colonel who flew in B-57's for Systems Command and later in B-52's before returning to SAC. He was highly decorated and was awarded the Distinguished Flying Cross for service in Vietnam. The patch displayed was worn on his flight suit while serving in SEA.

The pinched tube is very noticeable on this crutch-tip, and the tang runs up inside almost halfway to the end. The shape of the guard is rectangular and sometimes referred to as "squared-off" (at the ends). This blade is slender compared with some of the earlier Solingen's and is stamped *stainless* on the ricasso. Colonel Carlson has written, "The survival knife, for me, was and is a tool." Toward that end it was used and about ten years ago was sent to the Randall for "cleaning and touchup." This cleaning was nicely done and the knife hasn't suffered any from the "touchup."

The sheath is typical for the period, with small rivets, single piece construction on the back, and it carries a solid gray stone in the pocket.

Chuck Shipman Collection

MODEL 18-5½ PARATROOPER

Randall Made Knives offered name etching as a customer option. We see many examples of this on carried fighters and the neat block lettering and numbers often serve to identify that a knife was carried in a wartime theater of operations.

The etching on this "Attack-Survival" blade and guard was not done at the Shop, but was skillfully crafted and it certainly places the knife with a member of the US Army paratroopers during the "high-Vietnam" period of the war. The handle wrap adds to its legitimacy and the tube contents complete the package.

Dick Raynor Collection

MODEL 3-7 FIGHTER

The hunter grind on this knife has been modified in design by sharpening the top beveled edge, resulting in a "swedge," rather than a false edge. To finish the job, Randall attached a double hilt and the result is a fighter type with an upswept blade. Interestingly, the Johnson sheath is marked 1961 on the back, along with the name, which is also etched on the blade and *SO. EAST ASIA 1964-1968*.

The date 1961, if correct, is significant as it places production on the early side of "common wisdom" for Johnson Brown snaps (1962-1963). The other inscription puts the knife in that Theater of operations during the early years of the Vietnam buildup. We have presented the back of the sheath for reader viewing while the obverse side carries brown logo snaps and a two-tone gray stone.

Unfortunately, there are no accompanying specifics as to military use, so we rest our case on the circumstantial evidence presented; a "killer" of a fighter design and the inscriptions on the back of the sheath.

Dick Raynor Collection

VIETNAM ERA EBONY FIGHTER
"HE WAS IN A COMBAT OPERATION...."

The reality of war is driven home when a soldier's personal effects return with the deceased. Such was the case with the owner of this knife, an E-4 serving with the 23rd Infantry Division in Vietnam, who was killed in action on August 8, 1972. His casualty report simply states, *"He was in a combat operation when a hostile force was encountered."* A battle casualty, he commenced his tour in Vietnam eleven months earlier. The cause of death was a *"High velocity wound to the left chest and back."*

Little other battle information is available, although the soldier was a member of Co. E, 1st Bn. 52nd Inf. Regiment and the area of encounter was listed as *QUAN NGA*.

The fighter depicted here was part of the deceased's personal property and is officially listed as *"Knife with sheath."* As collectors we recognize the knife as a Model 1 with eight-inch blade and an ebony handle with nickel silver nameplate where his initials are prominently scrolled. The reverse side of the blade is etched with the owner's name.

Note the seven-spacer arrangement at the brass guard and the rear spacer stack. The blade grind appears to be very early 1960s. The knife looks to have been used, but it appears that it was not carried in the jungle in its accompanying original sheath.

Although this soldier's name is omitted here, the knife is accompanied by official records, which are now the property of collector, *Evan Nappen*.

5-SPACER MICARTA MODEL 2-8 GULF WAR

It is not unusual to have a knife that was carried in wartime predate that conflict. In fact, it was common during Korea, as well as the start-up years of Vietnam, that knives from a former war again saw service. In this case, this fighting stiletto, a gift from one brother to another upon transfer to the Middle East, was carried during the first Gulf war.

Lieutenant Andrew Fairchok was attached to the US 7th Corps, 244th RTOC in Saudi Arabia and fulfilled assignments throughout the desert around Hafer al'Batin and Wadi al'Batin while serving with a maneuver command. The knife accompanied him as part of his personal equipment.

The eight-inch stiletto was acquired used and represents 1970s production: note the five spacers. The micarta handle had become popular during this period, as well as the use of stainless steel. Note the width of the blade, emphasized by shallow choils, the result of blade redesign during the late 1960s.

The black sheath was a special order item.

Ron Frumkes Collection

GAMBLER – 4" MODEL

A variation of the previously introduced "Guardian," this knife produced for the same purposes reflects some subtle upgrades. The modified "dagger" with ricasso increases strength, while retaining its spear point and thumb serrations on the blade back. The handle material on this four-inch Gambler is maroon micarta with a rounded concave handle that is smooth throughout.

Some view this design as best utilized by placing the rounded butt into the palm of the hand and this style of handle is certainly more adaptable for that technique.

With these modifications to the knife, come some changes to the sheath as well; the most prominent being the addition of a large metal clip that allowed removal without unbuckling the belt.

The author has supplemented the original with a handcrafted sheath that provides for multiple-position carry including in the pocket, around the neck, and on the belt, much as its "Guardian" predecessor had.

Chapter Five
BOWIE KNIVES

The Bowie knife, made famous almost two hundred years ago through the exploits of Colonel James Bowie, was a fighter pure and simple. Long the domain of but a few antique collectors, it was nearly forgotten when the movie industry revived interest with the film *The Iron Mistress*. Bo Randall had, in all likelihood, built a few Bowie "types" along the way, but developed his line of "big fighters" after communicating with the studio and its actors and experts. Responding to a newly created demand, several designs were forthcoming that were authentically reproduced from historical reference and guidance from antique knife enthusiasts. There lies the difference between these Model 12s and the fighter and fighting stiletto of the previous decade.

We recognize that some of these models were carried in combat, and they are referenced in *Fighting Knives in Wartime*, but for the most part their massive size and cumbersome shape made carry on modern military field gear impractical. We approach this section then with that view in mind, and represent the several distinct types that Randall created with a historical theme, as no small part of the lasting appeal for these knives is their accurate and distinct design, crafted in the image of the original(s) created more than a century and a half ago.

SMITHSONIAN IVORY BRASSBACK

This is a big knife and probably modeled after an early "primitive," crafted by an American blacksmith, rather than one of those "fancy" Sheffield's exported to the frontier from across the ocean. Either way, it is impressive and owes at least some of its design influence from the experts who modeled the blade for *The Iron Mistress*. This knife is also early in the Randall development of this style and the handcrafting of a new model can be seen in many of its features. In the beginning the tips on the lugged hilts were brazed on as these are. The brass strip on the blade back was similarly attached and the process required skill. Note the thickness of the strip. The handle, with swelled center, is made from Shop supplied ivory and capped with brass. This early ivory shows the grain, which serves to enhance the age of the piece. All the spacers are of medium-thick size, with the standard colors used for other models.

A Clarence Moore sheath with red snaps is the scabbard for this "mighty" knife.

SMITHSONIAN PINNED IVORY BRASSBACK

We can compare this Bowie with the knife on the previous page and test our eye for common characteristics. They look the same. Note the brass strip, which is thicker still and extended a half-inch beyond the bevel, whereas the former stopped at the clip. The "welds" on the brass lugs can be more readily seen on this guard. The ivory handle has beautiful grain and is pinned to the tang, leaving nothing to interrupt the contour of the handle. Many of these Smithsonians were name etched, and this one is no exception.

What does seem to be typical for this model during the early years is the use of Moore sheaths. This one, unlike the previous knife, has brown opaque logo buttons.

PINNED IVORY BRASSBACK MOORE SHEATH

The handle on this Bowie has been shaped in a bit of a rectangle, providing a more comfortable and secure gripping surface in spite of the smooth material. I, for one, don't get tired of seeing Shop ivory, as each piece is just a little different in size, shape and grain. All the similarities consistent with this period are apparent in this knife; the blade having its original polish and showing visible signs of the forging process. This also extends to the accompanying sheath, which, like the knife, is absolutely unused despite a darkening of the stone pocket. The stone in the pouch is two-part gray.

PINNED STAG SMITHSONIAN HEISER SHEATH

Primitive and carried, this Smithsonian shows use, scratches and patina, but retains the full thickness of its blade. The handle is impressively shaped and is made from a beautiful piece of Stag. This material, procured for decades from India, is no longer readily available in either quality or quantity. Early pieces like this will some day be collectable just for this handle material. Note the pin, forward of center, which helps to fix the handle in place. This knife does not carry the brass strip on the blade back, which was an option, thereby creating a slightly different look overall.

We see another Moore sheath and this one appears to have been dyed. Translucent red snaps were used by Randall from shortly after WW II (1946) to perhaps 1950 on most models, but can be found on the larger Bowie sheaths up to several years later.

CAPPED STAG BRASSBACK WITH FINGER GROOVES HEISER SHEATH

This Bowie has a nicely contoured stag handle with finger grooves and was probably made during the mid to late 1950s. The contrast between the previous stag handle and this one shows some definite refinement in style. The brass strip is a bit thinner than those previously depicted and this continues to be a trend through the end of the brassback period. Note the little lugs on the brass hilt. They are noticeably smaller and not attached, but shaped from the guard itself. This may be one of the early attempts at this modification. This knife also has a hole drilled in the butt cap for a lanyard loop.

The sheath is a Heiser and has brown buttons. Compare the stone pocket flap with those Moore sheaths on Bowies previously photographed.

Accompanying the knife is a clay replica of a pre-Colombian Ecuadorian Indian death mask.

EARLY 1950s CONFEDERATE BOWIE MOORE SHEATH

This knife is the earliest leather-handled Confederate Bowie that the Author has seen. Notice how the "tucked-up" choil creates an image of a more primitive blade style as it tapers back into the thick brass guard. As with the previously depicted Smithsonians, the lugs on this early piece are brazed. This can be identified by the stubby uneven "tips" and by closely examining the base of the lugs where they were joined.

The polish is original, the forging process and the hammer left a "dimpled" blade, and the logo didn't get a clean strike. This is rough work, all original and very convincing. The solder is heavy and uneven, adding to the attraction of a knife of this period. Note the thick center spacer, short heavy handle and the thickness of the leather washers in comparison to the later Model 12-11 "Light" that follows in this section. The hex nut securing the butt cap is a large one with the protruding tang ground in the shape of a small dome.

Clarence Moore made the sheath. It is unmarked, but requires little study to identify. Beautifully made, it fits the knife snugly and has the translucent snaps that appear on many of the Bowie sheaths he crafted.

Photographed along with the knife is an interesting example of pre-Colombian statuary representing mythical idol "Pao-Los" nos Erectos.

CONFEDERATE BOWIE LATE 1960s

We can make some comparisons between this knife and the early Confederate Bowie previously depicted. This is more refined work and it is very good. Blade grind, guard and handle shape, in fact the entire knife, shows very careful attention to detail with the polishing perfectly done. Its unused condition is not uncommon for these big knives and this allows us to appreciate the workmanship that was so carefully completed over forty years ago. Note the shape of the lugs on the guard. The five-spacer arrangement is typical for this period, about fifteen years after the previously depicted Confederate was made.

The sheath is a Johnson, nicely made and with a white stone in the pouch. The return to the white stone, a bit softer than the two-part gray, was brief and seems to have been available along with a single grit gray beginning in the very late 1960s.

PINNED IVORY SPORTSMAN'S BOWIE MOORE SHEATH

As with the other Sportsman's Bowies featured in this section, choil-cuts have been made in the blades. Why? We don't know for sure, but it may just have been a traditional design feature. In any event, they soon disappeared on this model. Instead of the normal cut, the choil on this knife is "stepped" back to the guard and appears to have been a decorative innovation. However, it doesn't change the shape of the blade, which follows the grind seen on most Model 12-9s (exception(s) noted).

The handle has been nicely shaped into a swelled center and pinned in place. Further, ivory doesn't hurt the overall image of the Bowie one bit.

Take note of the subtle contouring of the accompanying sheath, which succeeds in complementing the knife in quality of craftsmanship.

Included in the photograph are early-pinned ivory Dominoes in a period box.

SPORTSMAN'S BOWIE WITH CAPPED IVORY HANDLE

Bowie customers had several options when it came to ordering a knife and the one in this photograph shows an ivory handle with escutcheon plate along with a coolie cap and collar in brass. The handle shape differs from the swelled-center "commando" style that evolved with the Model 2 in the 1950s, as seen displayed on the Sportsman's Bowie featured earlier in this section. This one is described as concave and lends itself to the style of embellishment incorporated into this fine piece.

For those collectors who favor a more practical style of Bowie, the nine-inch blade should help it to qualify.

The knife, with its Johnson sheath, was probably made during the late 1960s. They are photographed with a U.S. Gorget with twenty-four stars, circa 1825.

Dave Harmon Collection

MODEL 12-9 WITH LUGGED HILTS

The Sportsman's Bowie was introduced a few months later than the larger "heavy & light" Bowies, as they were referred to in the Shop. It appears to follow the lines of the Smithsonian, but on a reduced scale. Although many of the former were made with brass strips on the blade back, this is seldom the case with this model. The knife depicted here has a leather swelled-center handle, which was standard on most of the Bowie line unless otherwise specified. There are medium-thick spacers at both ends of the handle and a domed nut on the butt cap. The lugs on the brass guard are brazed and the entire shape reflects early handwork. The blade itself has a small choil cut that we can sometimes see on earlier Bowies, Smithsonians excepted. All of this tends to indicate manufacture in the middle 1950s.

The sheath is a Heiser, dark tan, very nicely made, sort of like a Moore and has brown snaps. The keeper strap is diagonal, which we see in greater numbers years later. The back of the sheath shows "corn-row" ridges, somewhat rare on a Bowie. These tooling marks extend to all of the underside(s) of the visible leather, as well as in the fold of the belt loop. The sheath is virtually unused, but has a leg-tie hole at the tip.

Jeff Saucier Collection

MODEL 12-9 WITH FIGHTER GUARD

This knife, along with the previously depicted Model 12-9, shares similar style leather handles, but is unlike it in the shape of the guard. The "fighter" hilt, standard on the Models 1 and 2, appears infrequently on knives of this size. It seems, however, that they were used on some of the first Bowie models crafted. The choil-cut is seen again, which is another indicator of mid-fifties production.

The bevel on the top line, running from the clip to the blade back, reveals a different grind and looks to be original on this knife. The sheath is a Heiser with brown button snaps and diagonal keeper strap.

The child's shirt in the background is from the nineteenth century and may have been made for a centennial celebration.

Jeff Saucier Collection

RIVETED SHEATH MODEL 12

Bowie knives should look the part and, if they were crafted during the Vietnam conflict, what is more natural than to order a micarta handle and a riveted sheath? This Sportsman's Model 12 was made during 1971 and is probably a rarity due to the accompanying sheath with rivets. It is a big knife no matter how it is viewed and perhaps that is why it shows no use, although many were reportedly ordered during the war and some have seen extensive use in Vietnam.

By 1970 most models in the line had been standardized in design and the Bowie depicted here exhibits those signs of refinement reflected in the grinding and polishing.

As with all of these types of sheaths, the shape is dictated by the requirement to punch rivets, and is unmarked by model and/or blade length. This well-made Johnson has the appearance of being indestructible, but has never been put to the test.

Dick Raynor Collection

THORPE BOWIE IN IVORY JOHNSON SHEATH

Here lies the model with the longest blade in the Randall line of knives. It looks like a short sword. Credit for period authenticity goes to the designer of the knife, Raymond Thorpe, who was recognized during the 1950s as an authority on nineteenth century Bowie knives. Robert Gaddis included original sketches of this style in his informative and well-researched book *Randall Made Knives, The History of the Man and the Blades*. Of all the models, this was perhaps the least popular, but did gain attention with a pairing that included the Arkansas toothpick in a presentation set made for King Faisal II of Iraq.

This "Thorpe" has a forward curved hilt, flanged scalloped collar and cap in brass and a nickel silver escutcheon plate without initials. The ivory is shop-supplied and shows typical checking and cracking for its age. Note the irregular handwork on the cap.

The sheath is a Johnson with nickel-plated snaps and a two-tone gray stone.

ARKANSAS TOOTHPICK IVORY

The image that Bowies have created is as varied as the many examples that were made. As the term has grown to become generic, it embraces all sizes and types. The six-inch Model 13 was introduced sometime after the original Randall "Toothpick" and was probably intended to be more ornamental than functional. This one has been decked out with ivory and a handcrafted cap and collar, which presents a stylish little knife. Although photographed individually, this is a companion to the previously depicted Thorpe Bowie of similar custom work. When photographed together, the two make an impressive set.

This knife is accommodated in an embossed leather covered document box, circa 1770, which also shows a scrimshaw powder horn from the same era.

KING FAISAL SET

In the past, the Randall catalog has carried a photograph of a Thorpe and a large Toothpick, similarly dressed, under the label of *Custom Made Knives*. Someone liked the idea, but substituted a small toothpick for the larger model. The original presentation matched set is famous due to the intended owner, King Faisal of Iraq. This one shows like appeal without the lineage.

The contrast in size is interesting and probably represents both the largest and smallest knives of this type, unified in appearance by the same style handle and guard.

It's a bit more difficult to accurately date knives without standard handles and spacers, but this pair was probably made during the mid-1960s as indicated by the sheaths and stone, not to mention the style of handwork in brass.

Photographed with this set is a Mesa Verde handled pot, circa 1100.

ARKANSAS TOOTHPICK MOORE SHEATH

It is difficult to determine whether the name "Arkansas Toothpick" originated from the shape of the blade or the region where knives designed like this were carried and used with deadly effectiveness. What is certain is that during the early nineteenth century all big knives were generally referred to as "Bowies" and they didn't draw the line in Arkansas when it came to banning them. This 1950s Randall Toothpick has a long (12") blade and probably resembles a traditional style in its primitive shape. Like all of the Bowies that he designed during the 1950s, this one has the distinctive lugged hilt and a commando shaped leather washer handle. The lugs are brazed-on, which can be identified by marks around their circumference. The butt cap was made of brass to match the guard. Note the stamp on the blade — small — to accommodate the size of the ricasso.

Clarence Moore crafted the sheath, the workmanship of which should someday be universally recognized for its superior quality and uniqueness of design.

For comparison, we have included in the photograph a Revolutionary War dagger, the blade of which was made from an American Pike or Spontoon. The knife has an iron guard and ferrule that is cast in one piece (rare). The hand-shaped and filed oak handle conceals the tang, the end of which is visible from the rear of the pommel.

WOSTENHOLM BOWIE
10" BLADE – IXL SHEATH

Most Randall knife collectors are familiar with Solingen blades that were made in Germany and helped to alleviate the increased demands on the shop during the Vietnam War. Those blades were not hand forged, but machine made and the reduction in cost was an option well received by many servicemen going to Southeast Asia.

A similar venture during the early sixties resulted in Bo buying finished "Bowie" blades from the famous Wostenholm factory in Sheffield, England, that were re-handled and sold by Randall Made Knives. This is such a knife. The blade measures ten inches in length and is suitably etched with the maker's mark and an interesting inscription to Colonel James Bowie.

Sheffield England was the world leader in the knife industry during the height of our national expansion and capitalized by manufacturing and exporting vast numbers of extremely well made Bowie knives to the new frontier.

However, this later business venture was of brief duration and produced fewer than sixty-five knives of ten-inch length before these blades ceased to become available.

Chapter Six
SETS

Visual comparisons serve to aid us in learning more about the subtleties in the development stages and evolution of the knives that we collect. Some choose to rely mainly on the sheath, as it may indicate specific time periods to the viewer. However, in the event that the sheath is missing, replaced or substituted, there is nothing left to focus on but the knife itself.

In this section, parings appear without their sheaths in order to provide greater image of the knives depicted and hopefully make for not only a more comprehensive photograph, but a visually pleasing one as well. In most cases each individual knife appears in another section of this book, or in some cases, in *Randall Fighting Knives in Wartime*, where it is accompanied with the maker's scabbard, original to the knife.

This presentation creates an opportunity for the reader to observe and compare knives on their own, in the various pairs, sets and groups of like models that are photographed within.

WORLD WAR II FIGHTERS 1943

We would recognize both of these as early 1940s fighters in spite of the visual differences, which include guard shapes, spacers and butt cap dimensions. The knife on the right was made before the other, but both have wrist thong links, although one is brass and the other steel. In spite of the time margins, which was probably not wide, the contrasts between them reveal the range of differences in hand crafted fighters as they evolved toward standardization a decade later.

WORLD WAR II FIGHTER PAIR

Bob King, the owner of this pair that was documented in section four, carried one of these knives while on active duty, and it has been in his possession for the past six decades. What makes them of special importance is the reliability of dates of manufacture. This provides us with the opportunity to make visual identification during that difficult and confusing period (1945-1946).

Early WW II fighters can be reliably identified by the flat-sided blade grind as well as the presence of a wrist thong "link" at the butt cap. There are other differences as well. Establishing a firm time frame for the introduction of the wrist thong hole, and the more pronounced blade bevels on these knives, is tricky.

These two knives were made about six months apart, with the knife on the left being produced first. What small differences appear could well be due to the individual art of handcrafting. The style is significant, however, and the images provide a benchmark for middle 1940s fighter types.

Courtesy of Bob King

FIGHTERS WITH 6" BLADES

Here are three knives that appear individually with their sheaths elsewhere in this volume. The six-inch fighter on the left has an early type thick handle, the mid-1940s knife in the center a necked down handle, and the 1950s blade on the right, a "commando" Model 1 style swelled-center shape. Note the nut sequence on the butt caps.

The blades present the same progression. The 1940s knife on the left has an abrupt clip, peaking well above the flat of the blade. The middle knife retains the "hump," but is of a less radical grind. The 1950s fighter appears to be more streamlined the full length of the blade.

There is also a noticeable difference where the blade meets the hilt. Beginning with the knife on the left that is gently beveled to the guard, to the middle piece with emerging but narrow ricasso, and ending with the knife on the right with pronounced ricasso.

Similar observations can be made regarding the choil cutout and the spacer arrangements. Apparently Bo Randall favored the seven-inch blade for his fighters, but the six-inch versions are a very useful all purpose length. The shorter blade gives a more abrupt overall appearance, creating more pronounced and noticeable differences for the observer.

STAG FIGHTERS WITH 7" BLADES
1950s

These "fighters" paired for this photograph, although both handled in stag, offer a good contrast in type. The knife with the butt cap is fuller throughout; blade, guard and handle. Both have a longer lower quillon, which is obvious from this angle. The finger grooves on the pinned stag fighter change both the appearance and handling characteristics of the knife. The bevels and choils appear the same in spite of the contrasting size.

Of the two, the pinned knife is harder to date accurately due to the absence of a nut, (or nut and washer). The sheath places it in the early 1950s. Knife two was made a bit later with domed nut and brown button Heiser sheath.

Either way if you like stag on a fighter handle, it would be difficult to choose between them.

MODEL 1-7 FIGHTERS 1950s TO 1960s

First glance reveals that two of these knives have seen some use, while the other has not. For comparison purposes, this set presents some interesting points. The knife on the left has a spacer configuration used with very early 1950s fighters, which is medium thick and thin with a wide center spacer. The center knife has medium red and white, with a wide blue center spacer and resembles that which was utilized back in the 1940s and reintroduced again during the early to mid-1950s. The third fighter displays the three medium-thick/two thin arrangement often associated with the 1960s.

Both of the earlier knives have a brass washer and hex nut at the butt cap, while the one on the far right is capped with a domed nut. The handle shape of the third knife is an indication of the period as well, with its shorter guard, neat solder and reduced fishhook choil. Note the style of the blade, which has a gradual drop to the clip when compared to the "fifties" — a change in the grind that is in contrast to both other fighters.

LEATHER HANDLED FIGHTERS MID-1950s TO MID-1960s

This three-fighter group photograph features all leather-handled knives covering a ten-year span. The blade on the left is mid-1950s and has five medium-thick spacers at the guard. The piece in the center was made during the early 1960s and carries three medium thick and two thin. The knife at the right was made in 1965. There are differences in all aspects of these leather-handled fighters, which tend to reflect the period when they were produced. For example, look at the handle shapes, choil cuts and blade grinds. There are similarities as well, reflected in the reduced size of the guard(s) when compared to the 1950s. This depiction helps to reveal the appeal of the handmade knife, for no two are exactly alike.

As you might expect, the sheaths accompanying these fighters are a Heiser with brown buttons and handle keeper, a Johnson with brown buttons and diagonal strap, and a rough back Johnson with nickel-plated snaps.

FIGHTING STILETTOS
1940s-1960s

Here are three contrasting designs of the stiletto spanning over twenty years. The first features a blade with a "fuller" and more or less standardized leather handle with wrist thong link. The second exhibits a more refined blade, with small stamp, fully shaped swelled center handle and a nut with washer on the aluminum cap, *without a wrist thong hole*. The third is a complete departure in all aspects; broad blade, narrow choils, wider ricasso with large stamp and Attack-style flat guard in stainless steel and micarta handle. The photograph serves to illustrate the wide-ranging modifications brought about to suit customers changing requirements over the intervening years. In fact, it reflects the attempt to make an "indestructible" fighting stiletto after the manner of the "Attack-Survival" models of the same era and to that end is convincing.

1950s MODEL 1-8 FIGHTERS
LEATHER, IVORY, STAG

The photo presented here depicts a study in (handle) contrast of these similar fighters of the same vintage. Although the handle material is different, the lengths are the same and represent the type being made at this time — early 1950s. The comparison extends to the length of the guard(s) as well. Non-leather handled arrangements carried seven spacers. Note the width of the center (blue) spacer, which is also indicative of this time frame. The leather-handled knife received an arrangement that first appeared during the early 1950s, was replaced later with five medium thick, and then reappears on brown button Johnson sheathed knives (or before.) This fighter was ordered and delivered during 1954.

The blades are similar on all three knives and, although not exact (they seldom were), quite clearly reflect the grind of that period. The most obvious points of comparison are the choil cutouts and the length and angle of the sharpened top clip. The butt caps differ, as brass nuts were used on brass caps while the more typical nut/washer arrangement for aluminum caps prevailed into the mid-1950s when the domed nut was substituted.

SET OF THREE
STAG-HANDLED FIGHTERS

The unused condition of these stag-handled fighters helps to make comparisons easier. Blades are unblemished so that the grind(s) are clearly distinguishable. The depth of the choil cut creates the most noticeable change in the appearance of the blade. The return to the shallow choil and wider ricasso made for more steel at the guard and, theoretically, a stronger knife. These examples range in dates from 1963, 1965 and 1950-1951, left to right.

Handle shapes are also very representative of each vintage in spite of the use of stag. Notice the short handle characteristic of the early 1950s knife, longer shape of the early 1960s and the pronounced "drop" by 1965.

1950S FIGHTER PAIR STAG WITH 8" BLADES

The description pertaining to these knives is detailed earlier in the book. As a pair they merit another look, for one compliments the other. Together they provide an image of mutually supporting weapons, specially hand-crafted to a high grade, catering to the special requirements of the intended user. As such, they were ordered early in the 1950s and have remained together ever since. Note the thick center spacers on both front stacks. The original owner had the foresight to carefully store both the knives and sheaths separately so that the intervening years didn't take their toll. Instead, they remain a lasting tribute to the shop man who forged, ground, and fitted the finished product.

IVORY FIGHTERS

Both of these knives appeared separately along with their respective sheaths in *Randall Fighting Knives in Wartime*. This section provides the reader with an opportunity to view them together and take note of the similarities and distinctions between them. Although seemingly identical, the knife on the left is the earlier of the two. The blade has a longer clip and sharper steeper drop and appears to be narrower than the other. Note the length of the guards on both fighters. The spacer arrangements appear, at first glance, to be identical. However, the earlier knife has a thick center spacer, while the other is of standard width. Both handles are relatively short compared to later fighters and they have been handled with "Shop Ivory," a Randall supplied customer option. The second knife has a domed nut in place on the aluminum butt cap, in contrast with the nut and washer (earlier) arrangement on the first. The two make an interesting set, similar in many aspects, but reflecting the differences that help to identify and early 1950s knife from one crafted later in the decade.

IVORY FIGHTER PAIR

There is a bit more to compare in this set of fighters than the previous two ivory Model 1-8s depicted in this section. The blades are similar in length and bevel and the solder is uneven on both. The guards show a difference, as the nickel silver knife is longer and more offset than the brass. The latter has a nice piece of ivory, beautifully contoured with good length and the normal 7-spacer stack with three thick at the butt cap. The nickel silver ivory-handled knife has grooved recesses for the fingers and is shorter than the other. However, its overall length is equal, due to the unusual addition of a unique spacer arrangement at the butt cap, where three thick spacers stretch the stack an additional 3/8 of an inch. Both butt caps are of the thin type with small steel hex nuts in place.

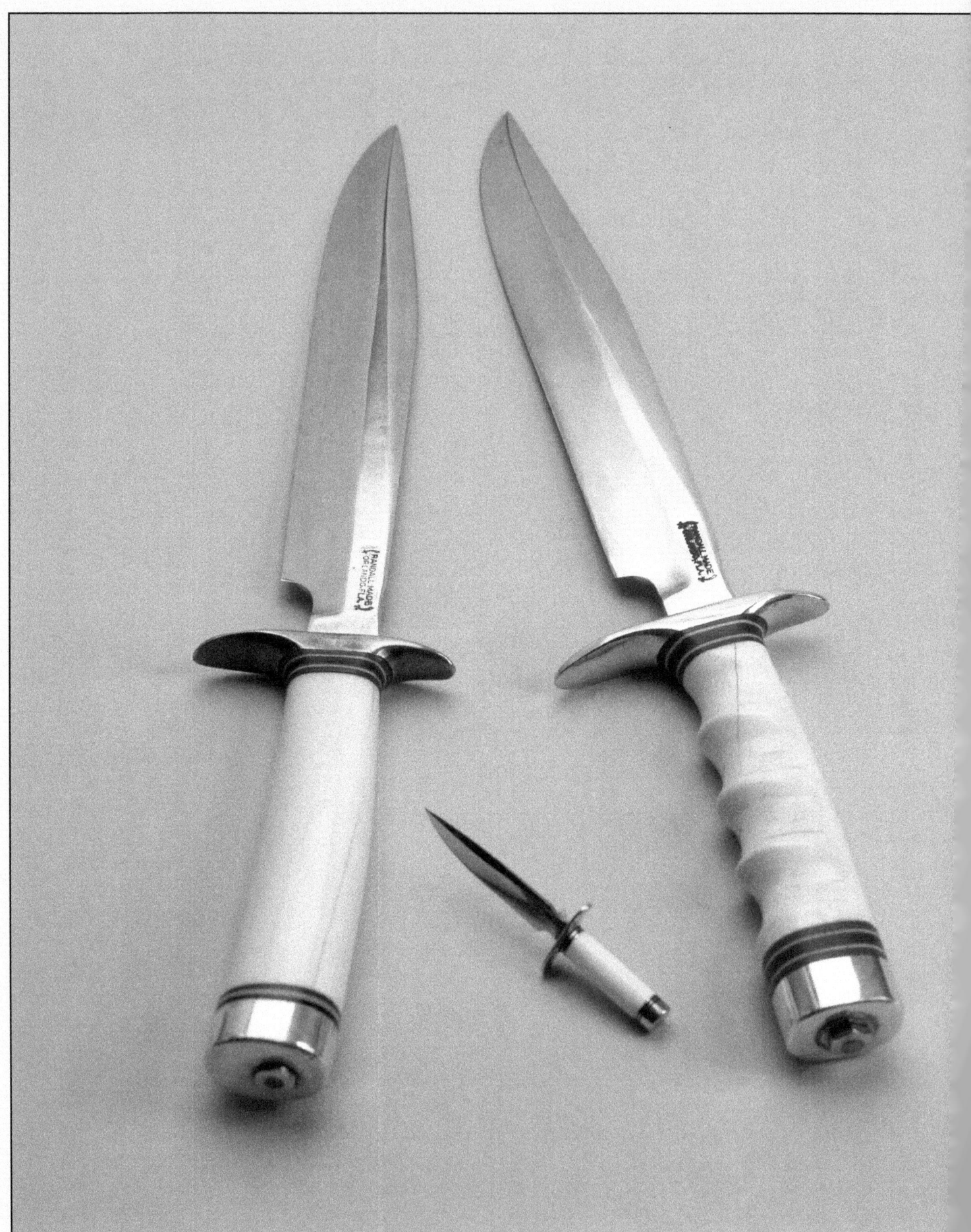

STAG FIGHTERS JOHNSON BROWN BUTTON SHEATHS

A well-preserved pair of early 1960s fighters carries over some of the more commonly associated design features of the late 1950s models, especially in the blade grind of the Model 1 and the shape of the Model 2 blade at the choil. This appears to be a matched set. Note the full and rounded stag on the stiletto and the grooved handle on the fighter, both of which were designed to enhance the type of grip that the contrasting blade styles demanded for their intended use.

The stag was secured without butt caps, which provides a bit more latitude in overall shaping, and are not pinned as they were routinely a few years previously. Spacer arrangements at this time were seven at the guard for non-leather handles, which is typical until the mid-1970s.

MODEL 14-7½ TENITES

The difference between these two "classic" tenite Model 14s becomes obvious when compared side-by-side. What we are contrasting is a Solingen-made blade on a somewhat earlier knife against an "Orlando Fl." blade on a knife that was made later. Besides the stamping, we can see design differences in the blades. The Orlando blade has almost lost the "hump" that was a prominent feature on the prototype models and which remained a feature on the Solingen ground blades until the end. Streamlining and refining blade shapes was, and still is, a method used to improve suitability overtime. The hump gave way to a level blade back, similar to the fighter that the Model 14 design was copied from. Don't overlook the guards for comparison.

When we compare handles we notice shallow flat-sided grooves on the Solingen knife, and chamfering at the edges, creating a "blocky" appearance. The Orlando knife has rounded edges more integrated into the handle, giving it a more finished look. Perhaps the most pronounced similarity to the careful observer is the extended tang. When these knives were first offered in the catalog, the wrist thong had a "slider" and the little adjustable tab is visible on both. Stainless steel did not begin to achieve popularity until the mid-1960s, so both of these knives were forged from carbon steel.

Choosing between the two knives is a personal matter. The knife on the left is unique in its top line. The knife blade on the right has achieved the unparalleled design features of the "fighting knife," while gaining in size and utility. For those who cannot make up their minds, do what the author did.

THREE TENITE AIRMAN

A very popular model during the Vietnam War, the Model 15, handled in tenite, was anything but universal in appearance. To some degree, the three examples here illustrate those differences, which appear in guard, handle and tang. The knife on the left has a handle representing an early type. Note the full, flat sides. The center knife has a more streamlined appearance in both blade and handle, while the "Airman" on the right is epoxied on the tang and shows no boltholes.

THREE TENITE DIVERS

The Diver is a model that doesn't vary in grind from knife to knife as much as the other full tang tenites. Perhaps the reason is that it was introduced later and development of the Model 14 and Model 15 took the more radical changes. Another reason is the spear-point design of the blade and, of course, the shape of the guard, the latter being a half-hilt by design. There are subtle changes that span about two years that can be seen in the width of these blades. We also see a difference in the blade cutout, just forward of the guard.

The tenite marked with "SS" on the blade indicates a date of manufacture somewhere about 1964, which is about when these choils were cut shallower. We recognize that the extended tang knife came first and this one, with its deeper choil cut, may have been a few years earlier. Stainless steel was not an option on early tenites and the double "SS" stamps were the first used in the Shop.

The epoxied tenite on the "SS" knife is a later material, introduced in an attempt to counter shrinkage and warping, and it was short lived. The third knife is handled in brown micarta and exhibits a wider blade. Together, these three provide a nice contrast to a pretty straightforward design. All three blades were forged in Orlando. Note the nickel silver guards, which are standard on the Model 16s. The Diver style, although not as popular a choice for ground troops, offers a nice option for those who favor a spear-point blade.

TENITE MODELS 14-15-16

Tenite was used as handle material on just three models in the Randall line – all full tang knives. Introduced sometime soon after the first prototype knives were built for the USMC, tenite survived for another ten years and became associated with the Models 14 and 15 then being carried in Southeast Asia. With the adoption of micarta, tenite, an injection plastic material, was discontinued and even replaced when servicemen's knives were returned to the Shop for cleaning or repair. Who could anticipate that this field-inferior green plastic would have such collector appeal in the future? However, it does, and depicted in this photograph are three period knives handled with tenite that represent, in the minds of many, the typical Vietnam Randall combat knife of the day.

Note the distinctive style of each: the large full blade and massive guard on the Model 14, the Model 1-like blade shape with smaller hilt on the Model 15 and the spear-point blade design and half guard on the Model 16 Diver.

1960s ASTROS

Of the full tang models, this knife has the distinction of being the least popular, in spite of the "Space Odyssey" that other similar knives were exposed to. There are some differences in the two presented here besides the variety and color of their respective handle materials.

Handwork can be viewed in the images, especially on the blades. The long guard on the black micarta knife is offset and angled. The handle on the brown micarta example is narrow and carries through to the blade as well. The reverse side of this knife blade is etched with the date, 1965. The other knife was most likely produced shortly afterwards. The grayish black micarta was an early variety, soon replaced by a more universal black, which became the standard. The sheath for this knife is a "Splitback" with small rivets — another indication of its approximate age.

Of course, the brown version is more collectible, due to its scarcity and the short duration that it was used as a full tang handle material.

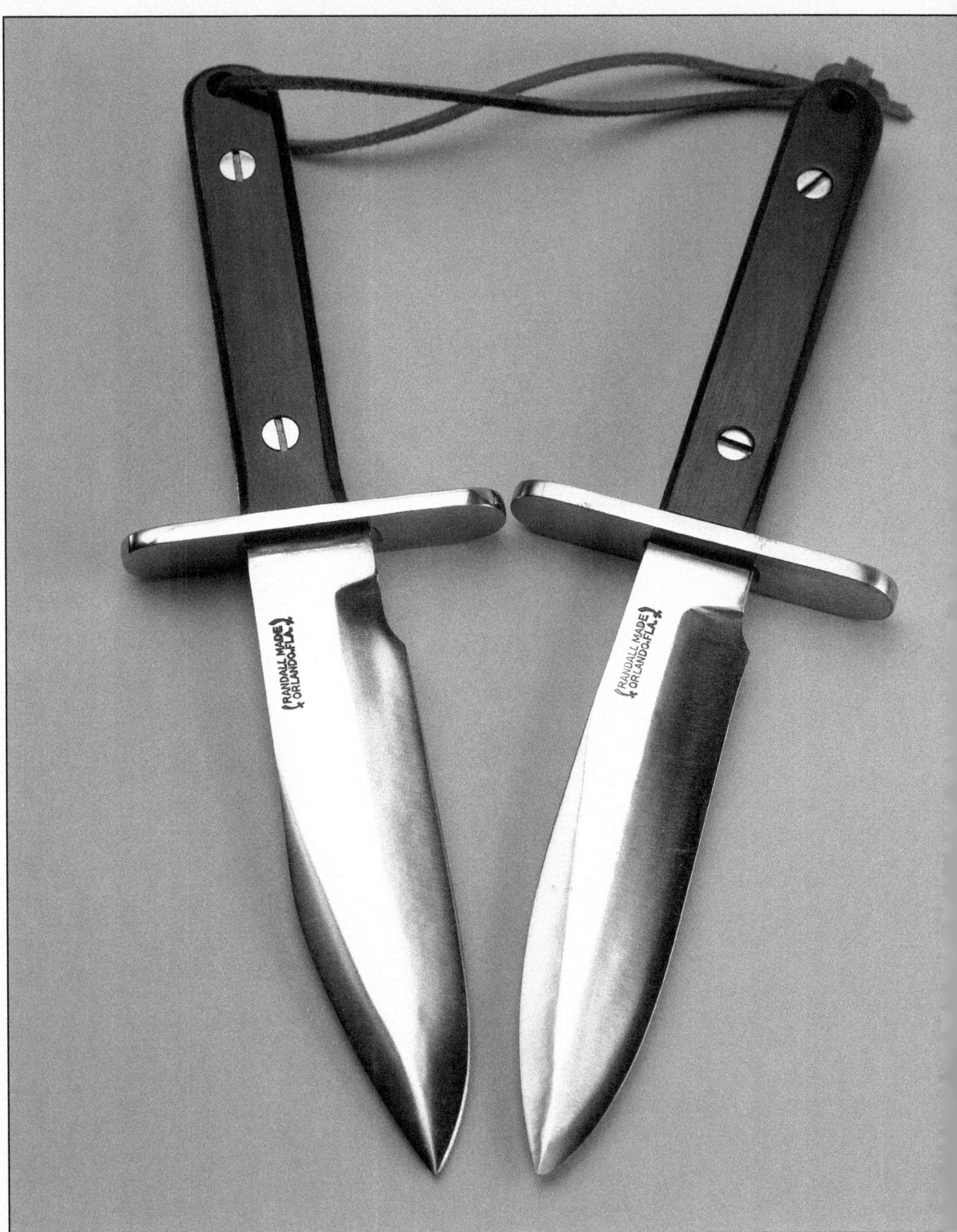

WORLD WAR II FIGHTERS

This group represents the World War II period of Randall "Fighter" production, while exhibiting some of the variance in individual knife crafting. Spacer differences are obvious, as well as the shape of the aluminum butt caps. The earliest of these knives shows the makers mark further forward on the blade. Note that all examples have a folded brass "tab" or "link" that form a pocket for the wrist thong.

Depicting knives without their sheaths serves to underscore the requirement of learning to identify (date) a blade when they are separated from the original, as is often the case.

MID-1940s FIGHTERS

These knives all exhibit somewhat later characteristics than the 1943 to early 1944 fighter. The latter featured a stout blade, longer guard, and thicker handle, and utilized a wrist thong link or clip at the butt cap.

The knives in this photograph share similarities, including the blade and handle shapes. The wrist thong hole, probably introduced in mid or late 1944, is in evidence on all five.

The knife on the left has seen no use and the marks on the blade are from storage. This allows us a good look at the blade grind at the time. The fighter to its right has a similar shape, which can be identified in spite of heavy use. The choil cuts are about the same on both.

Each knife depicted shows the "standard" spacer configuration at the guard, with the exception of the middle piece, which has a thick center spacer. Note the absence of a tang nut, which is identifiable on some butt caps in catalogs and other period photographs of the time. This butt configuration resulted from the procedure of peening over the tang and then grinding off the extension flush with the butt cap. The original sheath is with this knife (see *Randall Fighting Knives*, page 49) and has the look of late WW II or mid-1940s construction.

The next two knives (right) appear to be identical except for length; as blade shapes, choils, handles and even the rear spacers are the same. The original sheath for the end fighter has a translucent red snap on the keeper, first used in 1946.

Notwithstanding any lack of conclusiveness, this group reflects the "type" of fighter built during the period 1944-1945 (or so), and if nothing more, stands in contrast to the previously presented fighters crafted earlier in the war. When we factor in the abrupt stop in fighter production in late 1945, and the reportedly large quantity of built inventory of this model, we can speculate that knives of this design may have been sold to customers months or even years after being stowed in their finished state. It's unknown whether sheaths were in abundance at the same time and/or received the same treatment.

Since many carried pieces were separated from their sheaths, the over reliance on the sheath for the best or only certain method of dating is a flawed contention, which only serves to ignore the specific characteristics of period knife construction.

Chapter Seven
SHEATHS

In the eyes of some, the sheath makes the knife. This may not be so perceived in every case, but without the one, the other will be reduced in value; ask any collector. When depicting a knife together with its sheath in a single photograph, despite its visual appeal in large format, it is not always possible to create an image that will permit the reader to compare differences between like examples. We have therefore included a section on selected sheaths that should be instructive and serve to better illustrate the points of reference made in the general text of this book.

The over reliance on sheaths as a certain means of identifying or dating a knife from any given period suggests that most can accurately "read" the sheath. Serious students will acknowledge that dating a sheath (or a knife) requires some understanding of intervening time frames and the various aspects of manufacture that go into production. In short, this is just another piece of the puzzle and should be treated this way.

It is towards this end that we offer some selected examples in full page format, which we hope will bring visual recognition as well as interest to the reader and provide a reference for those who pursue this hobby and eagerly seek more information about the knives (and sheaths) that they collect.

EARLY 1940s FIGHTER AND FIGHTING STILETTO 1942-1943

Both of these sheaths carry very early Randalls and neither is marked with a maker's name. The sheath on the left has the details of a Moore: close fitting, edging on the stone pocket, belt loop and keeper, no throat rivets and a beautiful finish.

The other at first glance looks similar, in fact it could be a copy and perhaps it is.

It has seen some hard service. The snaps are the same, contouring similar, although keeper placement is different and the latter seems to be a characteristic of Southern Saddlery. The same assertion is made about the type and placements of the rivets —Moore on the left, Southern Saddlery on the right.

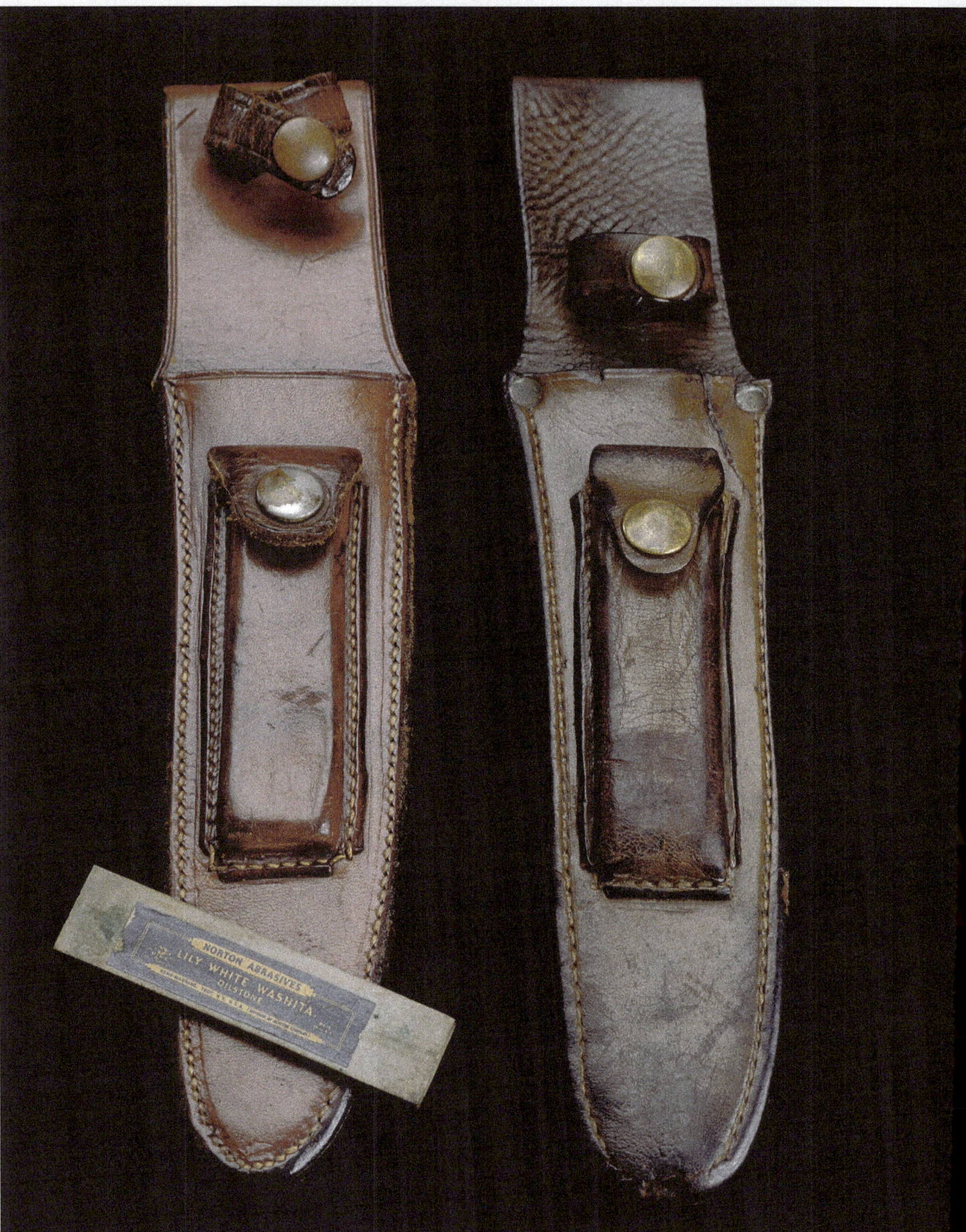

MODEL 1-8 SHEATHS – WW II

Judging by the knife that it holds, the Heiser on the left may be the earliest of the three. It shows C. J. Moore characteristics in the stone pocket flap and lack of throat rivets and even favors the shape of his sheaths of the time.

The center sheath is unmarked and, although in excellent condition, does not exhibit the workmanship associated with the former. It has been reported that Southern Saddlery became a supplier when they were able to secure snaps during war shortage. This one is most likely the product of that company from Tennessee, which furnished fighter sheaths during 1943 and 1944.

Notice the similarities between this and the sheath on its right. In all probability this Mosser, produced for Springfield Fighters, was a copy of the Southern Saddlery design, which accounts for the closeness in style if not quality.

The stones are original to the sheaths, the center stone fitting the pocket that was designed to accommodate its thickness.

MID-1940s HEISERS WITH HONING STONES

If exact dating is difficult, construction of these two sheaths is similar: rivets, stitching, contour, pocket size, keeper placement and back stamping. The finish work is a bit more detailed on the right hand Heiser, noticeably on the pocket flap and the edge of the belt loop. The latter was a later embellishment by Heiser, but could be seen on early Moores (and Southern Saddlery).

Other differences include the pocket flap and metal snaps on the left side sheath. The date of introduction of the logo snap is debatable, but it was certainly in use by 1946, if not before.

Based on these characteristics and on the knives which are depicted together with these sheaths in other sections of this book, it would appear that the sheath on the left is of earlier production.

1940s FIGHTER SHEATHS WITHOUT STONE POCKETS

If there is one "badge" of the carried knife, it may be the removal of the stone pocket on the sheath. Collectors who like such pieces recognize this practice as "field expediency." Obviously used, these three sheaths, all Heisers, have darkened with time. Although all were made during the 1940s, there are years between them. Note the stone pocket sizes where the stitching has been removed. The rivets are of three distinct types both at the mouth of the sheath and under the handle keeper. The sheath on the left accommodates the earliest fighter, the cover knife for *Randall Fighting Knives in Wartime*. The rivet at the tip, although somewhat flattened is the same type at the throat and is most likely the work of original production.

The center sheath, logo stamped on the front, has a metal snap like the first, but larger. This was made for a mid-1940s fighter.

The translucent button, or red snap, on the last sheath identifies it as mid to late 1940s production. It is stamped with a 7 on the back of the belt loop.

THREE MODEL 1-7
HEISER SHEATHS – 1950s

The first sheath, looking from left to right, is a very early 1950s Heiser made for a seven-inch Fighter. The stone pocket flap is wide and so is the keeper strap. The middle sheath is unused, which adds to the contrast, but they are almost identical in shape. The dark brown Heiser on the right has seen little use as well and displays a narrow flap on the pocket. This sheath carries a mid to late 1950s fighter.

The Heiser on the left has its original white stone, the others, two-part gray. Notice the dark stitching on the center sheath.

THREE HEISER
MODEL 1-8 SHEATHS – 1950s

The sheath on the left shows blade-edge contouring and a "flair" at the mouth. This is the earliest of the three. Its dark brown color may be indicative of Shop dye used during the period. It is simply stamped 8 under the Heiser logo and has a white stone in the pocket.

The middle sheath retains a hint of contouring on the back edge and a straight front edge and features a wide stone pocket like its predecessor, which carries a two-part gray. This one appears to be early to mid-1950s production. The final Heiser fighter sheath for a Model 1-8 is of mid to late 1950s vintage. It resembles the center sheath in overall appearance but has a narrow stone pocket flap.

MODEL 2-8 SHEATHS 1950s AND 1960s

The span of these three "Fighting Stiletto" sheaths is approximately fifteen years. The Heiser on the far left carries an early 1950s knife and has the typical wide stone pocket flap of that time. The center sheath with diagonal keeper, not incidentally a Johnson innovation, bares the brown snaps of the 1962-1963 period.

In contrast is a later Johnson sheath of heavier construction, supported by rivets. It carries the paracord ties of the mid to late 1960s. This depiction shows the gradual change in style and adaptation in order to accommodate "upgrades" such as security, strength and convenience of carry.

MODEL 2-9
STILETTO COMPARISON

We reference comments made in Section Two of this book regarding the center sheath appearing in this photograph. It is of early 1950s vintage, as is the Heiser on its right. A Clarence Moore sheath for a comparable model was not available for this photograph, due in part to Heiser's predominance at the time of manufacture (1950). Therefore we have used an early 1940s Moore stiletto sheath in comparable 8-inch blade length for this comparison, which appears on the left.

If Moore did not make (many) sheaths at this time, then what is the question? We know that Heiser received the bulk of the work after model "standardization" made production easier. This was not always the case, however, as Moore may have crafted his early sheaths from the finished knives due to variations in blade lengths.

By the time that this sheath was made, an eight-inch blade measured eight inches. But what about a nine-inch blade on a special order knife? The simplest solution would have been to task the local craftsman to make a "one-of-a-kind" sheath and the temptation is to accept this explanation. It may be correct.

We know that Moore made all of the early Bowie model sheaths in his distinctive style. In 1953-1954, they were new models and required special treatment until standardization when Heiser took over. The same reasoning that applies to the Bowies can be used to justify local crafting of the sheath in question. What about the obvious departure from type? There are precedents. For example, it appears that Moore mounted the keeper snap (button) on the left of the strap as it is viewed from the front *up until the Bowie sheaths were introduced,* at which time he changed over.

Heiser, on the other hand, appears to have always mounted theirs in the reverse; button on the right as viewed from the front.

This sheath offers a contradiction of type and is a worthy example to be submitted for collector scrutiny.

THREE JOHNSON 8" FIGHTER SHEATHS – 1960s

At first glance we notice the Heiser influence on the early Johnson brown button sheath on the left. A diagonal strap replaces the handle keeper that was formally used. The contouring is also reminiscent of Heiser's work.

The center sheath appears to have been made for a snug fit. The distinction may be partly due to the production date, perhaps late in the short cycle of Johnson brown buttons, as Maurice Johnson had then formalized his own way of doing things.

The chrome-plated snaps on the third example replaced the brown logo snaps. This sheath was made and delivered during 1965. All three are marked with the familiar Randall trademark on the rear of the belt loop.

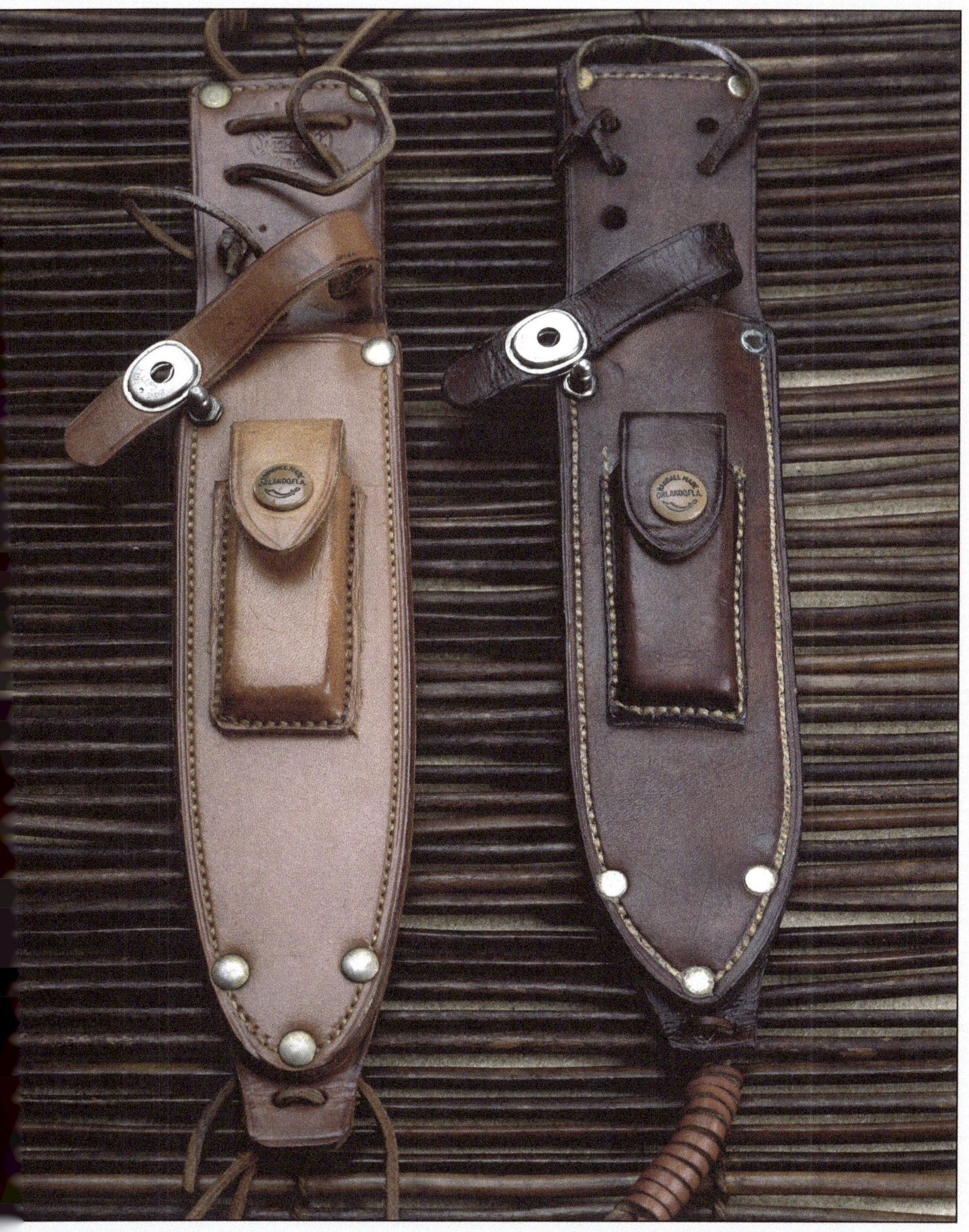

MODEL 14-7½ CANTEEN SNAP SHEATHS

A very early Heiser sheath in light brown or tan is shown on the left. The sheath was probably manufactured during the late 1950s and is in its original unused state. Notice the rivet type, which had evolved dramatically from a decade earlier, but still remains distinctive to a Heiser of this era. Compare to the rivets on the accompanying Johnson sheath to its right. In spite of some obvious differences (length) Johnson stayed with the Heiser design, that is, stitching, stone pocket and flap, although the maker's mark is on the back rather than the front of the sheath. Even the position of the studs and the tab length is similar. One of Johnson's first attempts at sheath making, these and other brown snap products were very true to the "original" design and reflect careful workmanship. Due to the comparatively few "lift-the-dot" sheaths that were manufactured, they could be classified as a rarity.

MODEL 15-5½ CANTEEN SNAP SHEATHS

The example on the left is an early Heiser, dyed black. The other is a Johnson that has also been dyed by the previous owner. Both are similar in type, with the Johnson stud moved up higher on the throat, thereby saving a rivet by replacing it with the stud and perhaps facilitating snapping in the process. This snap-type was short-lived in spite of the more durable fastener. Its failure to allow the knife to fully seat in the sheath may have been a factor in replacing the keeper with a button.

The Johnson in this comparison favors the Heiser sheath in all other characteristics and appears to be a very close period copy.

MODEL 18-5½ "CRUTCH-TIP" SHEATHS – 1960s

The type "C" sheaths depicted in this photograph span the 1960s and include, from left to right, a brown button with large throat rivets and splitback construction, steel snap version of the same sheath style, and a sheath with small rivets at the throat. All are Johnsons. Two of these sheaths carry the cord that was used at the time of manufacture. Johnson is the "sheath of record" for most collectors of the Model 18, as few Heisers were available during the Vietnam War. Once established, there were little variations from type to type with the possible exception of the splitback sheath with small rivets that was introduced and commented on in *Randall Fighting Knives in Wartime*.

SPORTSMAN'S BOWIE SHEATHS 1950s TO 1970

Clarence Moore's business relationship with RMK is well chronicled by Robert Gaddis in his work covering Bo's career as a knife maker. The peerless level of craftsmanship exhibited on his sheaths for all of the models deserves high praise and should be noted. The example depicted on the left in this photograph is a late sheath for Moore. It represents circa 1953-1954 production and still retains the tight contouring and careful finishing that became his trademark.

Bowies were introduced by RMK late in Moore's career as a sheath maker, but it appears that he got the early work until the various models became popular, eventually leading to HH Heiser predominance. The center sheath is a Heiser product that features a diagonal keeper strap to secure the knife in place. This was a recent innovation on 1950s sheaths, seen on the prototype models submitted to the USMC for testing, and on a few individual sheaths of various models prior to that. This sheath is also of excellent workmanship, although lacking the "individuality" of the former.

The Johnson sheath on the right, which utilizes rivets, was crafted during 1970. The return to rivets was made during the 1960s, coinciding with the Vietnam War and was an option on all models until discontinued by war's end. Contouring the sheath tips to match the blade style was not a prerequisite when placing a rivet. This applied to the width as well. Sheath size then was a product of the times as much as a reflection of individual maker characteristics, as each of these examples is typical of their respective craftsmanship.

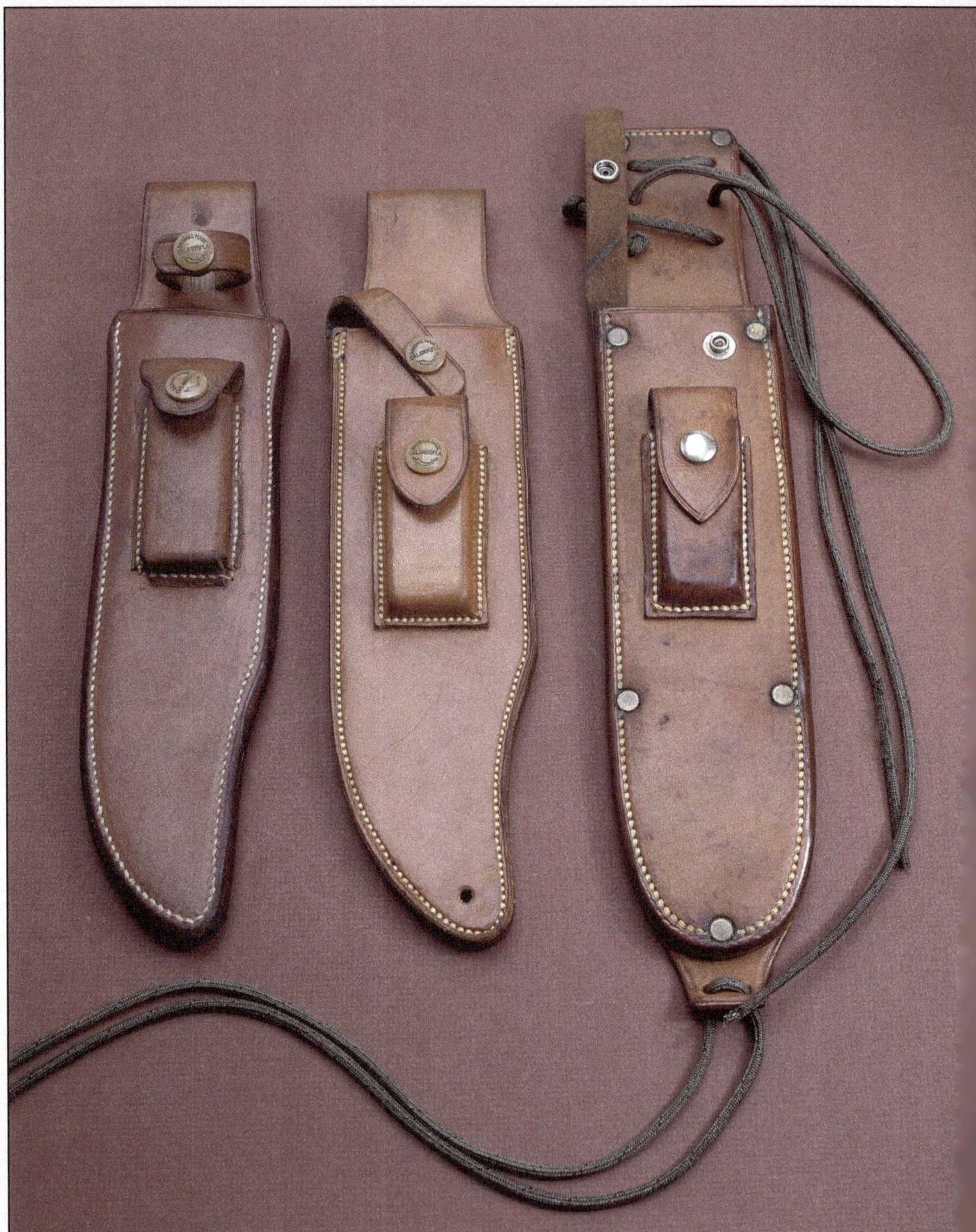

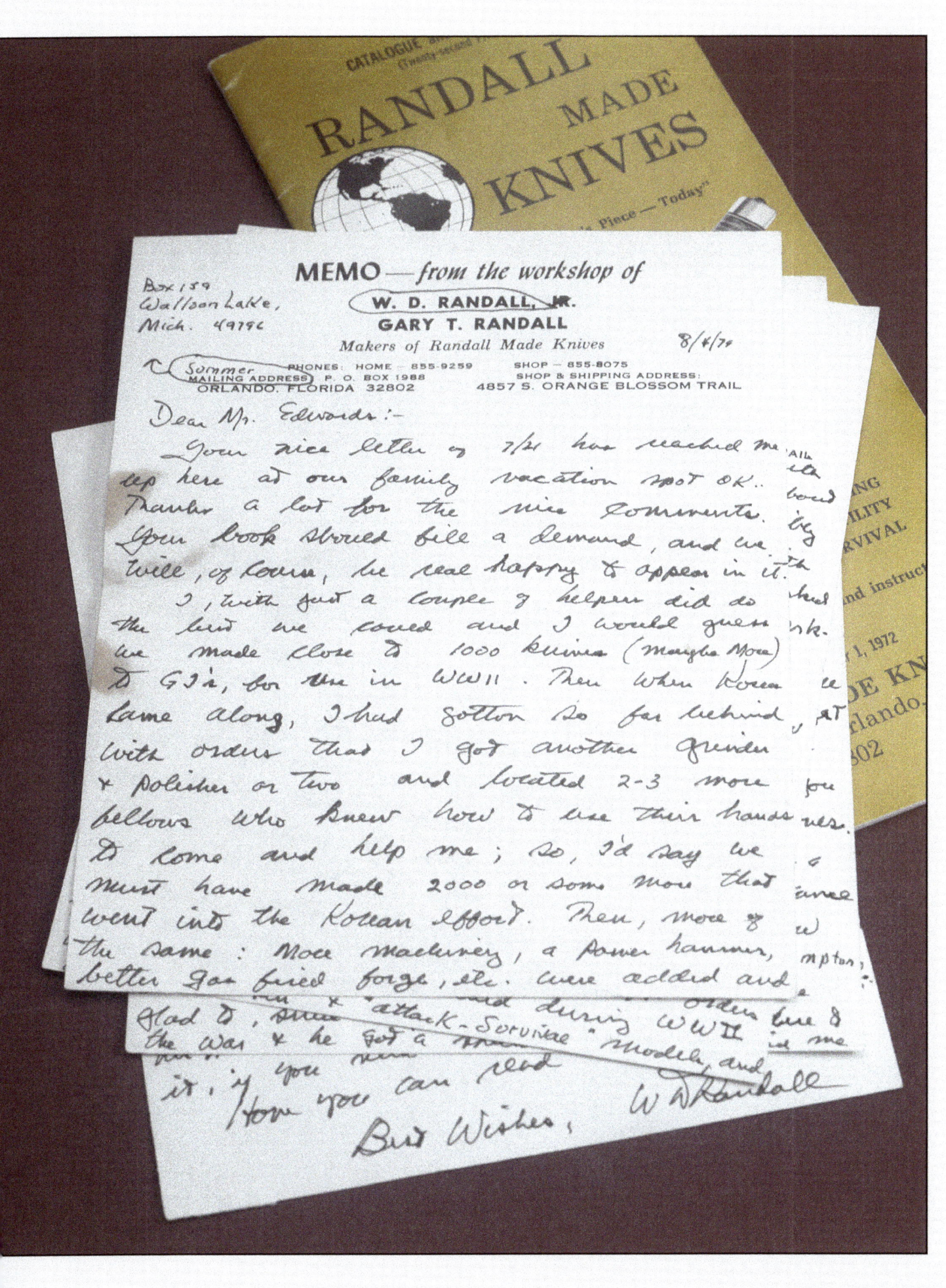

Chapter Eight
LETTERS

This section is devoted to the presentation of a number of letters written by W. D. Randall to John Edwards. The subject concerned John's inquiry regarding background on Randall Made knives. Edwards, a longtime military knife collector, was considering the publication of a book on the subject and was seeking first-hand information from several well-known makers and collectors.

The initial letter, written by John in July 1979, began a correspondence that spanned four years and included two dozen responses from Bo, on Randall letterhead and written in his own hand.

Beginning with some specific questions about WW II Fighters and gradually expanding into current knife production, Mr. Randall politely and graciously shared insights that were not then (or in some cases even now) public knowledge.

The year 1979 predated Robert Gaddis' fine book entitled *Randall Made Knives*, and Bo tested his memory and consulted company files in order to explain many of the events that John sought to clarify for his intended publication.

The letters are interesting and perhaps provide an insight into the sincere and generous character of the man who reintroduced the handcrafted knife to America at large, but this is not the purpose of their representation here. Only those pages that represent Bo's comments concerning Randall knife production and history are displayed for the reader.

Coupled with each written page is an accompanying photograph of a knife, sheath, or part thereof, inserted in order to illustrate a point being described in that portion of the letter.

It is my hope that seeing the original script will favorably impact the readers' perspective, as mine was, and thereby get an insight into the issue discussed without the use of artificial highlighting or the substitution of modern day fonts.

For the same reason, John's queries do not appear, as the replies speak for themselves. In some cases, one answer will beg another question, but that is out of the realm of this brief section. Coincidentally, much more information is available to the collector who has a thirst for knowledge on this subject today.

Finally, let me thank and congratulate my friend John Edwards for his generosity in making this material available and secondly, for his foresight into the knife-collecting world that lead to their preservation and eventual publication.

BO'S LETTER AND WW II MODEL 2-7

Correspondence between Bo Randall and military knife collector John Edwards of Springfield, Massachusetts, took place for more than a decade. Edwards was pursuing his interest in WW II combat knives and planned to publish this information: letters passing between the two reflected Bo's responses to John's queries about fighter models. The letter in this photo, taken with an early 1940s Fighting Stiletto, is revealing in that it reflects Bo's personal recollections of the sequence of development of his knives during the early WW II period.

The Model 2 was to become the second most popular fighter in the line. Perhaps that was the reason that when model numbers were ascribed, it was designated number 2. (The reader can draw his own conclusions). This letter and others have been made available to the author and represent first hand recollections prior to any large-scale publication on Randall knives forthcoming over a decade later.

We are indebted to John Edwards, a friend and longtime collector of military knives and militaria.

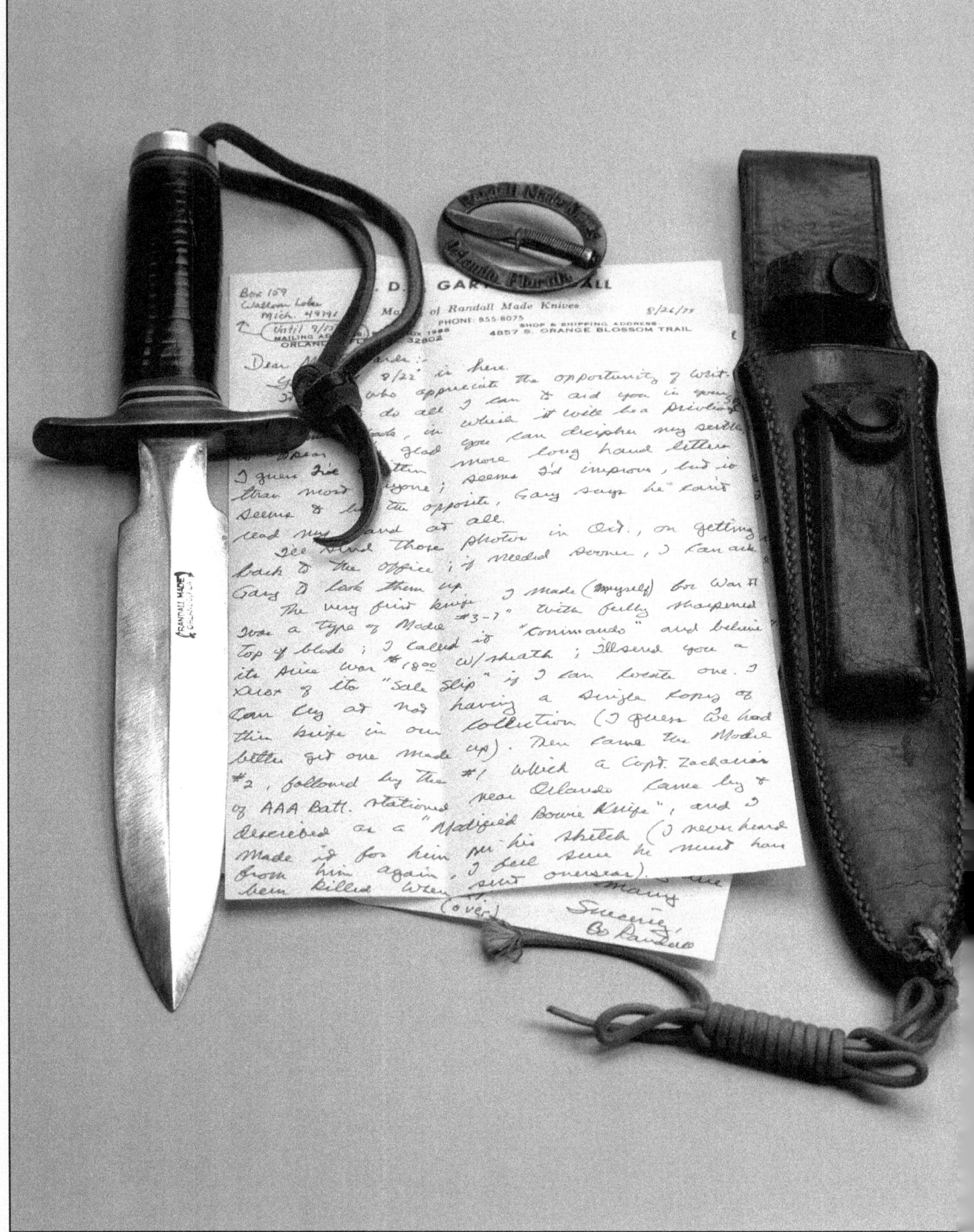

W. D. & GARY...
Makers of Randall Made Knives
PHONE: 855-8075
SHOP & SHIPPING ADDRESS:
4857 S. ORANGE BLOSSOM TRAIL
MAILING ADDRESS: P.O. BOX 1988
ORLANDO, FLORIDA 32802

Lake
49796

Dear Mr. Edwards:—

Good to have yours of 9/6.

We, at the shop, can fairly well tell the difference between the Early & Current Models #1, 2, & 3. The changes are subtle and more too prominent is so an ordinary person would have a hard time of it and we (at the shop) can only guess within 5-8 years. The very First #1½ x #2½, made almost 100% by myself, are recognizable by the recessed bent brass with hole drilled thru that I had & use for attaching the wrist thong; these are not very many of these around.

The Models #14 *... ...* several times; the developed at ... ... #15 evolved; ...
... ... specifically for USMC Pilots & ... ... was supposed to be short, strong & ... comp... ... wearable on arm or leg or boot. #14 (large version of #15) was my own id... ... for a properly strong knife for the ground troops (easily adaptable for Bayonet) with adaptation of proper fastner device). Of course, never expected to make the knives for the USMC or any Dept. of Government must ...

ORLANDO, FLA

BO'S LETTER AND
MODEL 1-7 WITH THONG LINK

Visible just above this early 1940s fighter handle are the comments in Bo's handwriting:

. . . The very first #1's & 2's, made almost 100% by myself, are recognizable by the unusual bent brass with hole drilled through I had to use for attaching the wrist thong; there are not many of these around.

The reference refers to the bent brass link (some were also made from steel), which serve to assist collectors in dating knives from this period. Of equal interest is the beginning of the sentence. This letter, dated September 1979, was sent from Walloon Lake, Michigan, and signed, *Bo Randall*.

BO'S LETTER AND SHEATH WITH EARLY FASTENERS

The sheath depicted with this 1980 letter to collector John Edwards belongs to the author and was depicted in *Randall Fighting Knives in Wartime* in Section 1 (reference the *Kressley Knife*). It was made by Clarence Moore and should be among the earliest that he constructed. The unclasped snap on the stone pocket shows a "glove-snap" type, but of large size. The keeper snap, painted brown, uncommon in 1940s sheaths, clearly depicts a different type not dissimilar to those finally adopted by RMK in 1963 when Johnson, who had just began making sheaths, upgraded the snaps. Perhaps this was the subject of Bo's comments in the letter displayed in this photograph, when he states:

. . . We did use a fine fastener, back before 1945, called "amzo," supplied by the big United Carr Fastener Corp.; it was a real fine and strong type.

There are no markings on these well-constructed sheath snaps. The Southern Saddlery sheath that is original to the Model 2, depicted elsewhere in this book, has identical snaps, both top and bottom.

MEMO — from the workshop of
W. D. RANDALL, JR.
GARY T. RANDALL
Makers of Randall Made Knives

PHONES: HOME — SHOP — 855-8075

Summer— MAILING ADDRESS

7/20/80

We did use a fine fastener back before 1945, called "Anzo", supplied by the big United Carr Fastner Corp.; it was a real fine & strong type. Actually! we have yet to see: The perfect fastener.

Bt.159
49796

Mr. John J. Edwards.
48 Worthington St
Chicopee
Mass.,

SPRINGFIELD FIGHTER AND BO'S LETTER

There's enough speculation about the Springfield Fighter to fill a book, but here in Bo's letter, he comments on the projects beginning and then goes on to qualify John's Fighter as a "*collector's piece*." Since then, some twenty years later, a good many Springfield owners would agree with that sentiment. The reference to Northampton Cutlery is revealing, as Bo's comments seem to bear out the author's contention that they were the first cutlers involved in the project. The number 500 is significant due to the fact that accurate reporting by Larson has been disputed; but this figure would be difficult to alter due to the records keeping requirement placed on a well-established company doing government work during wartime. Secondly, the 500 would refer to the output of Northampton *only*, but can be interpreted to quantify the "best-crafted" fighters produced in this project. Up until this time we could only hazard a guess. For a Springfield Fighter enthusiast, it indicates a known number for the high-grade knives that we collect. Work done after Northampton Cutlery was forced to desist is another matter.

The knife in the photograph represents a more-or-less typical grinding (fitting and finishing) of one of these early Model 1 copies. We have addressed the subject of workmanship in other material including in *Randall Fighting Knives in Wartime*.

The sheath is typical within the construction and color variations that surface with these fighters. The snaps are occasionally brass, as seen on this sheath, or black or metal painted black or brown.

BO'S LETTER AND HEISER SHEATH WITH BROWN OPAQUE SNAPS

An essay on sheath snaps, included in *Randall Fighting Knives in Wartime*, defines for the reader the author's view of the continuity of their introduction and use. This is *not* an exact science. In response to an inquiry by John Edwards twenty-five years ago, Bo readily identifies with the "opaque" brown logo snaps and the mid-1940s. He is clear on the point and it is indicated on the page produced here. Bob Gaddis, writing for the RKS newsletter, Issue # 33, also comments on the "first logo snaps" and, in finality, draws the same conclusion some years after this letter was written. The contention that the 'red' translucent snap was first has not been born out, notwithstanding subsequent research by Gaddis in the very important book on Randall and his knives, which supports an early appearance of these red logo buttons.

The sheath depicted here is most probably a mid-1940s (1945-1947) model and carries the brown button referred to as opaque. Red translucent snaps seem to be first encountered during 1946, and may have been a replacement for depleted opaque stock.

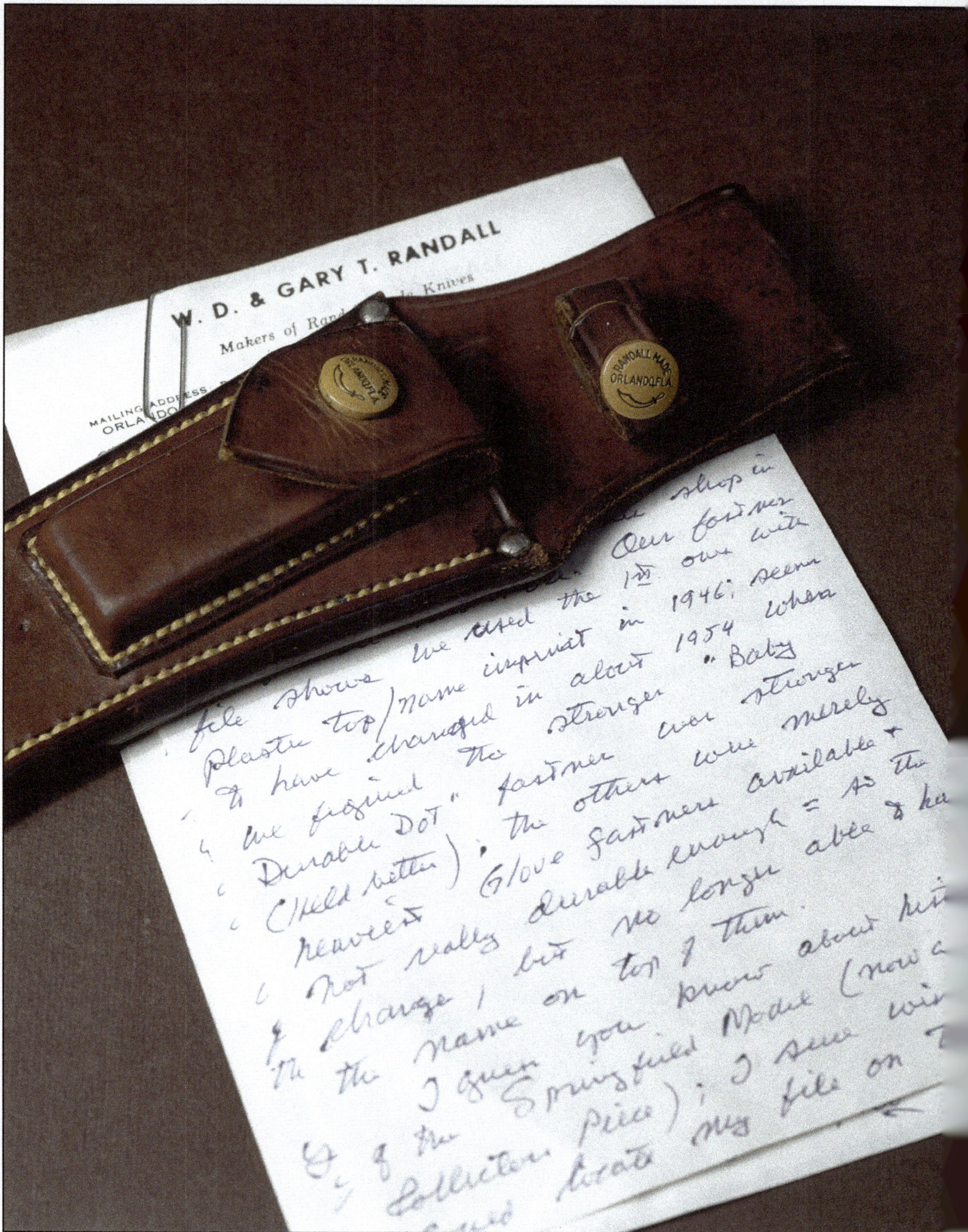

BO'S LETTER AND MODEL 14 "ATTACK" FOR GROUND TROOPS

In my view, what is most revealing in these letters are the candid statements that Bo has made in response to the questions asked him in correspondence that we are not viewing. I particularly like the one highlighted herein, beginning with:

The #14 (larger version of the #15) was <u>my</u> own idea for a properly strong knife for the ground troops (easily adaptable for bayonet use with adaptation of proper fastener device.)

In light of the history of this design, this is an understatement of significant proportion.

LETTER FROM BO
VIETNAM BOWIES

I have wondered about the relative suitability of the "Bowie class" knife for modern combat applications during the Vietnam War. Introduced in the early 1950s, the Smithsonian achieved a great deal of collector popularity. The Sportsman's Bowie, with nine-inch blade, followed soon after and it is to this knife that we look as possibly filling a combat role. Two such pieces appear in *Randall Fighting Knives in Wartime*; one with documented carry by a USAF fighter pilot.

Randall's comment in the accompanying letter removes any doubt about Bowie orders from servicemen during the conflict and opens up the field for military collectors to research documentation for these oversized "fighters." In retrospect, we realize the impact of the Randall Catalog on personal knife selection; i.e., the Model 4s when featured on the cover in the early 1950s. Subsequent writings drew similar attention to these big knives as well, and probably accounts for the statement made by Bo in the letter photographed. Again, we present this for the consideration of the reader and allow him to draw his own conclusion(s).

W. D. & GARY T. RANDALL

Makers of Randall Made Knives

PHONE: 855-8075

MAILING ADDRESS: P. O. BOX 1988
ORLANDO, FLORIDA 32802

SHOP & SHIPPING ADDRESS:
4857 S. ORANGE BLOSSOM TRAIL

That was the 1st time I'd ever even heard of a Bowie knife; I made quite a lot of them for GI's stationed around Orlando — a lot of them were training "Night Fighter Squadrons". No one ever actually asked for a Bowie knife to be made, until the advent of Movie "Iron Mistress", then everyone wanted a Bowie + even more so when the TV "Scott Forbes Jim Bowie series" came out. A lot of GI's carried Bowies in Vietnam, despite their bulkiness.

[...] to research history and go back to their 1st. use in the U.S. (I assume you know of my friend Wm. Williamson, of Santa Barbara, Cal., who is the world's leading authority on Bowie knives).

We didn't get many (if any) knives back from "addusses" during WWII, probably due to our not sending out so many back then.

Let me know what's next.
(over)

Sincerely,
Bo Randall

RONALD REAGAN

SUITE 812
10960 WILSHIRE BOULEVARD
LOS ANGELES, CALIFORNIA 90024

December 2, 1975

Mr. Walter Doane Randall
Post Office Box 1988
Orlando, Florida 32802

Dear friend Randall:

What a surprise and treat to hear from you after these many years. I do still have my knife and it is in good shape. It is still my pride and joy. You are a tempter though to send the brochure. It is by my bed for enjoyable bedtime reading (and drooling).

Thanks very much for the contribution. I'll forward it to the committee and thanks too for your generous words. I'll try to deserve them.

Best regards,

Ronald Reagan

RONALD REAGAN

CATALOGUE and KNIFE MANUAL
(Twenty-second Printing)

RANDALL
MA
KNIV

"Tomorrow's Collector's Piece —

RENOWNED
THROUGHOUT
THE WORLD
Established 1938

W. D. Randall, Jr.

100% HAND-MADE

For Every Purpo

HUNTING • FIGHTING
SKINNING • CARVING
DIVING • THROWING

Containing descriptions, price
for making

Prices effective Novembe

RANDALL MAD
P. O. Box 1988, Orla
32802

RONALD REAGAN LETTER
MODEL 1-7

By now most readers will have become acquainted with Randall's "Western salesman," but that was WW II *stuff*. This letter, from the future President, was written two wars later in 1975, and indicates the continued interest and enthusiasm that he had for Bo's handmade knives. It represents one very small insight into the mind of the man and is part of the Randall legacy.

Depicted along with the letter is a WW II Fighter, undoubtedly similar to the first Randall knife ordered by the future President of the United States.

INDEX

Randall Commando – WW II Fighter 8

Springfield Fighter – Wide Blade 10

Springfield Fighter 12

Springfield Fighter – Serial Number on Sheath..14

Model 1-7 Fighter – Mid-1940s 16

Mid-1940s Model 1-7 Fighter – *Russell H. Palmer* 18

Little Commando 20

1940s Model 5-6 22

Early 1950s Model 1-7 24

Early 1950s Model 1-8 Stag..26

Model 1-7 Stag with Compass – Heiser Sheath..28

Early 1950s Model 1-8 – Finger-grooved Ivory 30

1950s Brassback Fighter – Heiser Sheath..32

1950s Model 1-8 – Leather 34

1950s Model 1-8 Commando Stag 36

Model 1-7 – Lugged Hilt 38

Early 1960s 8-inch Fighter – Stag..40

Model 1-8 Stag – Double "SS" Stamp..42

1960s Model 1-8 – Low "S" – Walnut..44

Early 1960s Model 1-7 – Unmarked Leather Sheath....................................46

Vietnam Era Model 1-8 Stag Fighter 48

Model 1-6 – Delrin Handle 50

1943 Model 2-8 – Double-stamped Moore Sheath 54

1950s Model 2-7 – Pinned Stag..56

1940s Fighting Stiletto 58

1950s Model 2-8 – Ivory 60

1950 Fighting Stiletto – 9-inch Blade 62

Stag Model 2-8 – Early 1950s 64

1950s Model 2-7 – Pinned Stag – Heiser 66

Model 2-6 – Ivory – Modified Sheath 68

Stag Fighting Stiletto – Early 1960s 70

Double "SS" Model 2-8 – Ebony – Early 1960s 72

1960s Model 2-8 – Leather 74

Model 2-8 – Wide Commando Handle 76

Model 24 Guardian – *The Smallest Stiletto* 78

Model 14-7 $^1\!/^2$ Tenite – Orlando Blade 82

Brown Micarta Model 14-7 $^1\!/^2$ 84

Brown Micarta Model 14-7 $^1\!/^2$ 86

Model 15-5 $^1\!/^2$ Tenite – Johnson Canteen Snap............................88

Model 15-5 $^1\!/^2$ – Extended Tang 90

Model 15-5 $^1\!/^2$ – Name Etched 92

Model 15-5 $^1\!/^2$ – Epoxied Tenite 94

Model 16-7 – Tenite Diver..96

Astro – *Space Odyssey*...98

Early 1960s Astro – Brown Micarta Handle 100

Model 18-7 1/2 "Attack-Survival" – Full Tang Knife 102

18-7 $^1\!/^2$ Crutch-Tip with Handle Wrap.......................................104

Model 18-7 $^1\!/^2$ – Separate "S" – Black Sheath............................106

18-7 $^1\!/^2$ Solingen – Carbon Blade..108

Model 18-7 $^1\!/^2$ – Experimental Tube 110

Model 18-5 $^1\!/^2$ Crutch-tip – Orlando Blade 112

Mid-1960s Orlando Blade Crutch-Tip 114

Model 2-7 $^1\!/^2$ with Fuller 118

WW II 7 $^1\!/^2$ " Fighter with Heiser Sheath...................................120

WW II 8" Fighter – *Etched USMC* – Southern Saddlery 122

WW II Model 2-7 Fighting Stiletto – *Etched "Cook"* 124

World War II Fighter – 10" Blade 126

WW II 6" Fighter – *Gordon Palmer, USAAC* 128

World War II Fighter – *The Raid at Cabanatuan* 130

Mid-1940s Model 1-6 – *Name Etched "Hadwin"* 132

World War II Fighter – US Army Air Corps 134

World War II 8" Fighter – US Army 136

Saltwater Fishing Knife – *WW II UDT Operations* 138

Early 1950s Model 1-7 – *Korean Era* 140

Model 1-8 – Commando Handle – Korean War 142

Korean Era Commando Handle Fighter 144

Late 1940s Model 2-7 – Riveted Sheath – *Right of Passage* 146

1950s Model 2-7 *"Courage isn't written about . . . ."* 148

Tenite "Attack" – Moore Sheath 150

Guard-etched Model 14 – Heiser Canteen Snap 152

Tenite Model 14 – *Special Forces Airborne* 154

Brown Micarta 14-7 $^1/^2$ – *Hufnagle USMC* 156

Brown Micarta Model 15 "Airman" – *Hoagland* 158

Model 16-7 Brown Micarta – *Royal Canadian Air Force* 160

Model 18-7 $^1/^2$ – *USMC SNIPER* 162

Model 18-7 $^1/^2$ – *One Hundred Missions* 164

Model 18-5 $^1/^2$ – *Paratrooper* 166

Model 3-7 Fighter 168

Vietnam Era Ebony Fighter – *"He was in a combat operation . . . ."* 170

5-Spacer Micarta Model 2-8 – *Gulf War* 172

Gambler – 4" Model 174

Smithsonian Ivory Brassback 178

Smithsonian Pinned Ivory Brassback 180

Pinned Ivory Brassback – Moore Sheath 182

Pinned Stag Smithsonian – Heiser Sheath 184

Capped Stag Brassback with Finger Grooves – Heiser Sheath 186

Early 1950s Confederate Bowie – Moore Sheath..188

Confederate Bowie – Late 1960s 190

Pinned Ivory Sportsman's Bowie – Moore Sheath..192

Sportsman's Bowie with Capped Ivory Handle..194

Model 12-9 with Lugged Hilts..196

Model 12-9 with Fighter Guard..198

Riveted Sheath Model 12..200

Thorpe Bowie in Ivory – Johnson Sheath..202

Arkansas Toothpick – Ivory 204

King Faisal Set..206

Arkansas Toothpick – Moore Sheath..208

Wostenholm Bowie – 10" Blade – IXL Sheath..210

World War II Fighters – 1943..214

World War II Fighter Pair..216

Fighters with 6" Blades..218

Stag Fighters with 7" Blades – 1950s..220

Model 1-7 Fighters – 1950s to 1960s..222

Leather Handled Fighters – Mid-1950s to Mid-1960s 224

Fighting Stilettos – 1940s-1960s 226

1950s Model 1-8 Fighters – Leather, Ivory, Stag 228

Set Of Three Stag-handled Fighters 230

1950s Fighter Pair – Stag with 8" Blades 232

Ivory Fighters..234

Ivory Fighter Pair 236

Stag Fighters – Johnson Brown Button Sheaths...238

Model 14-7 $^1/^2$ Tenites 240

Three Tenite Airman ... 242

Three Tenite Divers ... 244

Tenite Models 14-15-16 ... 246

1960s Astros ... 248

World War II Fighters ... 250

Mid-1940s Fighters ... 252

Early 1940s Fighter and Fighting Stiletto – 1942-1943 ... 256

Model 1-8 Sheaths – WW II ... 258

Mid-1940s Heisers with Honing Stones ... 260

1940s Fighter Sheaths without Stone Pockets ... 262

Three Model 1-7 Heiser Sheaths – 1950s ... 264

Three Heiser Model 1-8 Sheaths – 1950s ... 266

Model 2-8 Sheaths – 1950s and 1960s ... 268

Model 2-9 Stiletto Comparison ... 270

Three Johnson 8" Fighter Sheaths – 1960s ... 272

Model 14-7 1/2 Canteen Snap Sheaths ... 274

Model 15-5 1/2 Canteen Snap Sheaths ... 276

Model 18-5 1/2 "Crutch-tip" Sheaths – 1960s ... 278

Sportsman's Bowie Sheaths – 1950s to 1970 ... 280

Bo's Letter and WW II Model 2-7 ... 284

Bo's Letter and Model 1-7 with Thong Link ... 286

Bo's Letter and Sheath with Early Fasteners ... 288

Springfield Fighter and Bo's Letter ... 290

Bo's Letter and Heiser Sheath with Brown Opaque Snaps ... 292

Bo's Letter and Model 14 "Attack" for Ground Troops ... 294

Letter from Bo – Vietnam Bowies ... 296

Ronald Reagan Letter – Model 1-7 ... 298